W. Robertson Nicoll

The Return to the Cross

W. Robertson Nicoll

The Return to the Cross

ISBN/EAN: 9783337252823

Printed in Europe, USA, Canada, Australia, Japan

Cover: Foto ©Lupo / pixelio.de

More available books at **www.hansebooks.com**

THE RETURN TO THE CROSS

BY THE REV.

W. ROBERTSON NICOLL, M.A. LL.D.

Editor of "The Expositor" "The Expositor's Bible"
&c.

NEW YORK

DODD MEAD & COMPANY

149 & 151 FIFTH AVENUE

1897

TO MY WIFE

CONTENTS

	PAGE
THE SECRET OF CHRISTIAN EXPERIENCE	9
FROM THE TABERNACLE TO THE HOUSE	41
THE VALUE OF PECULIAR POSSESSIONS	53
THE LONG LOVE OF CHRIST	69
THE SORROWS OF THE SAVIOUR	79
"A LISTENER UNTO DEATH"	89
THE WISDOM OF GOD IN A MYSTERY	97
THE PRAYER MEETING	109
"IF TWO OF YOU SHALL AGREE"	119
THE CASTING AWAY OF THEOLOGY	129
IS THE GOSPEL OF CHRIST FORGOTTEN?	143
"CAST YOUR DEADLY DOING DOWN"	155
IS CHRIST DEAD IN VAIN?	167
"BEING LET GO"	179
"THEY WITHOUT US"	187
THE WEIGHT OF THE ENDS OF THE WORLD	195
THE BACKWATER OF LIFE	205
THE SCHOOL OF TYRANNUS	213

CONTENTS

	PAGE
THE MOTHERS OF ST. PAUL	221
FROM GLORY TO GLORY	229
GIVERS AND RECEIVERS	237
CHRIST WAITING TO BE GRACIOUS	245
"WOMEN RECEIVED THEIR DEAD"	251
THE THEOLOGY OF LITTLE CHILDREN	261
THE EVANGELICAL LOVE FOR CHRIST	273
THE THEOLOGY OF WALTER PATER	285
IS THE SERMON ON THE MOUNT THE CHRISTIAN GOSPEL?	297
"GEOCENTRICISM": THE LATEST SCARECROW	309

THE SECRET OF CHRISTIAN EXPERIENCE*

IN his most beautiful book, "Grace Abounding," Bunyan speaks as follows: "Upon a day the good providence of God did cast me to *Bedford*, to work on my calling; and in one of the streets of that *Town*, I came where there were three or four poor *Women* sitting at a door in the sun, and talking about the things of God; and being now willing to hear them discourse I drew near to hear what they said, for I was now a brisk talker also myself in the matters of religion. But I may say *I heard, but I understood not;* for they were far above, out of my reach. Their talk was about a new birth, the work of God on their

* Address delivered at the close of the Session, Theological College, Bala, July 1, 1897.

hearts, also how they were convinced of their miserable state by nature. They talked how God had visited their souls with His love in the *Lord Jesus*, and with what words and promises they had been refreshed, comforted, and supported against the temptations of the devil. Moreover they reasoned of the suggestions and temptations of Satan in particular; and told to each other by which they had been afflicted, and how they were borne up under his assaults. They also discoursed of their own wretchedness of heart, of their unbelief, and did contemn, slight, and abhor their own righteousness, as filthy and insufficient to do them any good. And methought they spake as if joy did make them speak; they spake with such pleasantness of Scripture language, and with such appearance of grace in all they said, that they were to me as if they had found a new world, as if they were people that dwelt alone, and were not to be reckoned amongst their neighbours." You observe the characteristics of this experience. These saints were conscious of the love of God in Christ Jesus. They were conscious of the defences they received against the assaults of the Wicked One. They were conscious also of their own wretchedness of heart and unbelief, and did utterly contemn, slight, and abhor their own righteousness. And the result and outcome of this mixed experience was an exuberant joy, and such an appearance of grace as made their hearer desire a place among them. They appeared to him to have found the new world. It is this combination of joy and wretchedness that has to be explained. In a day when ethical preaching prevails, in a day when some profess to have found a perfect victory over sin, and others not less loudly speak as if sin should permanently darken the believer's life, it may be well for us to ask whether the experience of these women of Bedford is not the normal and apostolic type, whether it is true that in the end our best righteousness is to be utterly contemned, slighted, and abhorred, whether it is true that to the last we must speak of our own wretchedness of heart and unbelief, and whether in spite of all this we may not rejoice in God through our Lord Jesus Christ.

I

In the first place what is supremely important to a minister is that he should have a message. Other things are by no means to be despised. He should be taught how to express that message in the speech of his day, and in its relations to the varying aspects of thought. The vindication of theological colleges is mainly to be found in this necessity, and nearly all wise Christians are of opinion that the education of preachers, so far from being lowered, ought to be made much more thorough than it is. Melanchthon in his day and Westcott in ours have specially brought out as against pietists that Christianity is appointed for the transfiguration of the human in every department, that the worlds of science and art and literature are accessible to the mind of Christ, and that the crowns of these kingdoms also should be set on His royal head. But I do not think it is needful to dwell on this, but rather to insist on the other side that the preacher without a definite message, no matter how well furnished otherwise, is necessarily impotent. Rely upon it that the people of Wales, who have listened to the noblest pulpit eloquence in the world, do not ask from you secular teaching. As time passes they will ask for it less than ever. It is by slow and piecemeal deepening of the great divine thoughts that the spring of life rises and abides in our churches.

No teaching that is purely ethical or intellectual, or the result of the exercise of the human reason, will do other than lay waste the supernatural Church that is redeemed by the blood of the Lamb.

Further, this message is always a secret given by the Holy Ghost, and blessed by the Holy Ghost. No book, no earthly teacher, can ever impart that hidden wisdom without which your ministry must be a thing of nought. You must in your inmost souls live through the struggle and the victory. Nothing avails at all in this connection except an immediate and original experience of salvation. Dr. Dale has told us how, when he was a mere youth, on his knees and in keen distress about his personal salvation, he first read through the "Anxious Inquirer." "Night after night I waited with eager impatience for the house to become still, that in undisturbed solitude I might agonise over the book which has taught so many to trust in God." It is through anguish and fear for the most part, and always through anxiety and eagerness, that we are led to that quiet trust in Christ in which we find rest and strength, and through which we are enabled by the Holy Spirit to teach other souls to forsake sin and live for God. I ought to say that the Christian secret is with us a secret that has to be told. We are not with Newman, who denounced the practice of preaching the Atonement to the unconverted, who declared that the preacher should connect the Gospel with natural religion, and mark out obedience to the moral law as the ordinary means of attaining a Christian faith. We stand with St. Paul, who delivered first of all that Christ died for our sins according to the Scriptures, and rose again on the third day.

Again, we accept apostolic doctrine and apostolic experience as normal. Of the attempt made in our time to disparage the teachings of the Apostles, in favour of the teaching of Christ, I will only say that when we are done with the Gospels we are not done with Christ. One might imagine from certain writers that the subject of one part, the golden part, of the New Testament was Christ, and that the subject of the remaining part was some one or something else. You know that it is otherwise, that the Apostles, rightly or wrongly, spoke of nothing but Christ. They used the intensest expressions to describe their relation to Him, that relation of utter humility, obedience, trust, worship, intimacy, which almost passed into complete identification. They speak without a doubt not only of the Christ of Palestine, but of the Christ who died and rose again. They profess to know through the revelation of the Holy Ghost the far-reaching significance of Christ's death. More than this, they claim to have penetrated the veil which hides the risen Lord in heaven. They profess to know how He fulfils His office as a minister of the sanctuary, and of the true tabernacle which the Lord pitched, and not man. Now I have simply to say that their claims are either true or false. On these subjects no man may speak without the spirit of revelation. All human imaginings and suppositions are as idle as the chattering of sparrows. We have therefore to say either that we have no light, that the so-called revelation may be cancelled, that we must not concern ourselves with it, that we must content ourselves with the imitation of our Lord's earthly life, or else we must admit that the Holy Ghost glorified Christ by taking of His and showing it to the Apostles. What is not competent is to sit in judgment on what is either a revelation or a deception, and try to part it into false and true. The Apostles must in the nature of the case be trusted all in all or not at all. What we know is that when Christian doctrine has been made a living thing, when swelling hearts and conquering souls have been subdued by the divine grace and mercy, it has been by those who, like the reformers, gloried in being scholars of the Apostles.

Once more, in discussing these subjects, in maintaining that there is a normal Christian faith, we are not judging those from whose theology we dissent. If St. Paul himself said "we prophesy in part," surely all of us may say the same thing. There are those who have laid passionate hold on certain aspects of the faith to the neglect of others, who lived in the very household and court of God, and at whose feet we may well sit in great humility. What we must say in such cases is, "He appeared unto them in another form." In His full-orbed glory Christ appears to His people's hearts as their representative and their substitute, the priest and the victim. But there are those to whom He is rather a personal friend, one to whom they turn in hours of need for inspiration and succour. They know Christ after this manner, although they do not know Him perfectly. Still, it is the business of preachers of the Gospel to seek after the full Gospel of the full Christ, and to mark divergences from it even when they thankfully admit that these divergences have often been used by God for the clearer understanding of His truth, and for the rescue of Christian doctrines which were in peril of obscuration.

II

Let us now turn to the Christian experience of the Reformation, and inquire how far it conformed with that related by Bunyan. In the endlessly instructive spiritual history of Luther we find that with him, from first to last, justification by faith was the article of a standing or falling Church. Everything, he said, was contained in it that he taught and urged against the devil through his whole life. What was it that led Luther to this great truth, and what did it experimentally mean for him? It meant the satisfaction of the else unappeasable inquietude for sin which drove him from the Church of Rome. If he had been seeking peace with man or peace with the Church, his object would have been attained with comparative ease. But he was seeking a far greater thing. He was asking for peace with God. He knew that this peace was not to be found by grants from the Church, or by the accumulated merits of his ascetic practices. He needed something that would atone for the guilt of the past. He needed a righteousness which of himself he could never attain. He found in Christ the true oblation and satisfaction for his sins. He found that in Christ he was delivered from all guilt, that Christ does with our sins just as though He had committed them, and therefore they are swallowed and drowned in Him. One of the great errors of modern evangelicalism has been to identify justification with pardon. Justification is more than pardon. It means something that is done once for all, and the shelter of which falls alike upon past, present, and future. It does not mean simply that the believer is restored to the favour of God, and that the penalty of the law is remitted. It does not mean that Christ's work rendered the remission of sin possible. It means that the believer is delivered from condemnation by the satisfaction of the law, and that the law no longer condemns, but acquits and pronounces just. Any doctrine short of this deprives the life of peace. We receive in justification the present and unchangeable forgiveness of sins through the blood of the Atonement. Great is the message of forgiveness, and I should not deny but far rather maintain that it includes more than is commonly imagined. Who, it has been asked, can put into words intelligible to the mere understanding what it is that he seeks when he says "Forgive"? We can say only what it is not. We are sure only that none who from his heart has breathed the prayer, whether into a divine or human ear, has ever meant by it merely "Remit the due penalty, help me to escape suffering." What he does mean it is impossible perhaps to put into other words, but we may be certain that it is something that none can confer who cannot also condemn. Justification is more even than forgiveness, and justifying faith is not mere faith in an impersonal word of Christ, but a confiding resignation in the living Christ as Reconciler. In Him faith lays hold of high-priestly love. The Christ who brings us justification enters into living relation with us. He enters in through the dark soul's door, and the Lord sups with His children, and they with Him. We cannot originate the new life or confer it on ourselves. We discover it in Christ, to whom we are united by the faith that justifies. Faith, as is said by Dorner, involves love, and good works are present in principle. There is a logical but not an actual severance between justification by faith and that union with Christ which is the source of sanctification. It is the union between man and Christ that makes Christ the propitiation, and without such a union we could not have the remission of sins. It is also through this union with Christ that we attain His likeness. It is not merely that Christ influences. It is not that the heart turns resolutely from evil and the world of darkness, and dares the toil and the endeavour by which it attains the world of light. It is not that Christ acts upon us as one soul acts upon another. Wordsworth says that the mission of the poet is to add sunshine to daylight, and we have all known those spirits in whose neighbourhood thought seemed clearer, feeling stronger, the whole being stimulated and vivified. But the Apostles were not satisfied with that. They knew that not in that way could these dim, infirm, half-blinded natures be conformed to the image of the Son. It was true that the passions and the forces of their life were drawn to Christ. But that was not enough. In the spiritual order

Christ is the vine and we are the branches. The life of the vine is active in all its members. Christ in the fullest sense is related to us, for we are rooted in Him, and our true life is lower even than our deepest consciousness. It is not on our own resources, enriched as they may be through divine grace, that we rely; it is a deeper depth; a depth to express which language is taxed and exhausted. The fact is no less than this, that the springs of our life and power lie outside of ourselves in Christ, are independent of the changes in our personal condition, and furnish us with a joy and a strength which it is out of our power to understand or account for save as we know that His infinitude is under our finitude, that we are rooted in the Eternal Son.

Now that we have put together those two doctrines of justification by faith and of union with Christ, what is the result? Is it an experience of unmixed serenity and triumph? No. There is one relation, our new covenant relation to God, which continues well ordered in all things and sure. Through all changes in the life of the Christian it remains the same. The righteousness of Christ has been imputed to us, that righteousness which God's righteousness requires Him to require, and who shall lay anything to the charge of God's elect when it is God that justifieth? But it is otherwise in our own personal conflict with sin. The life which is joined to Christ has for its instrument an organisation which is disordered and impaired. Defects of intellect, weaknesses of the body, and an imperfectly disciplined conscience obstruct the perfect manifestation of the grace and beauty and strength of the divine life. The new nature is fiercely assailed by the world, the flesh, and the devil. More than that: when we discover our union with Christ we are oppressed as we never were by the feeling of our own imperfection, of our own infinite distance from God. The nearer we come to God, the greater seems the interval between His righteousness and our unrighteousness. The sense of sin grows as the sin itself diminishes. It aches, and throbs, and burns in the heart. We utterly contemn, slight, and abhor our own righteousness. We have rejected it, cast it away as the ground of our justification before God, and after justification it appears further and further from the divine thought and ideal. Besides, though God forgives us, we do not forgive ourselves. The pain of old sin burns through all the fog of the past even when we are loosed from our past in His own blood. What, then, is the relation of the righteousness of faith to the righteousness of life? It is this—that the consciousness of peace and even joy in God is perfectly consistent with a consciousness of sin not only not vanishing, but even becoming more intense. Fellowship with Christ by faith and the faithfulness of Christ come up and atone for our imperfection before God, and are the pledge and seal of our ultimate perfection. And so comes that strange life which believers know, the humiliation of ill deserts with the assurance of God's love, the sense of unworthiness with the sense of peace, happy confidence with humble self-distrust, the self-renunciation and the self-abasement which gleam and burn through all the writings of the Apostles, and which make the normal Christian experience.

III

I propose next to say something about the evangelical revival and the controversy between William Law and John Wesley. The study of

William Law has lately been renewed among us, mainly by the labours of Dr. Whyte. His works have been reprinted in a cheap and complete form, and another divine justly honoured by the Evangelical Church, the Rev. Andrew Murray, has followed Dr. Whyte in publishing a selection from Law's books. No competent judge can doubt for a moment Law's intellectual greatness, his acuteness in argument, his power and charm of style. His was also a very high and leading religious mind, religious, perhaps, rather than Christian. It is with diffidence that one dissents in any way from those who have lately brought Law's works before Christian readers. But it is fair to say that since Wesley's time evangelical theologians have looked askance at much in his writings, and I venture to think justly. Law is what may be called an extra-biblical writer, in this respect resembling John Foster and differing from John Bunyan. Bunyan's writings are saturated with the Scriptures. He says himself, "I was never out of the Bible," and his mind fastened upon it "as a horse-leech on the vein." Law like Foster gathered a few great ideas from Scripture, and both used their powerful faculties for the illumination and enforcement of these.

Law does not quote the Bible very frequently, nor very correctly, and he assumes the right of interpreting expressions which do not suit his system in a sense peculiar to himself. In that very striking book, "The Penfolk," Mr. Gilmour describes for us a disciple of Law who says: "I dinna often quote frae Scripture, for it is like a fiddle; ye can play ony tune on it to people." Law evidently held the view, described by Robertson Smith as the essence of rationalism, that revelations of God are given additional to the Scripture. He said of Wesley that he and the Pope were under the same necessity of condemning and anathematising the mystery of God revealed by Jacob Böhme. Law's theology is extremely difficult to characterise justly, and I venture to think that the existing attempts in this direction are unsatisfactory. You have first of all to remember that he to a certain extent altered his positions from time to time, never so far as I know admitting any great change of opinion. What is far more difficult is that he continually uses scriptural and theological language in a sense of his own which may very easily be misunderstood. I think it would be difficult to draw a perfectly consistent scheme from Law's books, to reconcile, for example, his doctrine of apostolic succession and the sophistical ribaldry on the Invisible Church which are to be found in his letters to the Bishop of Bangor with his letters to a lady who proposed to join the Church of Rome. But on certain points he is clear, and these points are so vital to evangelicalism that I cannot understand those who can see no ground for Wesley's criticism. Let me give a few quotations. "The one only work of Christ as the Redeemer is to raise into life the smothered spark of heaven in you." "The atonement of the divine wrath and justice, and the extinguishing of sin in the creature are only different expressions of the same thing." When Wesley complained that Law grounded nothing on "faith in His blood," Law replied, "What is faith in His blood but a hearty willingness and a full desire wholly to cease or turn away from all heathenish or Jewish practice?" Writing against the doctrine of justification by faith alone, Law triumphantly quotes from Christ's words at the end of the Sermon on the Mount, "Whosoever heareth these sayings of mine and doeth them, I will liken him unto a wise man who built his house upon a rock," the rock according to Law being not the saying, but the doing of the sayings. In fact, he goes so far as to say expressly that when St. Paul speaks of works as unprofitable for salvation he means only Jewish or heathenish works. In his later days he used to speak passionately against the idea of there being any such thing as the wrath of God. When confronted by the overwhelming Scripture testimony he coolly replied that the expressions were all figurative, and yet he speaks in the most orthodox way of Christ being the atonement and satisfaction for sin. One has to read him carefully and closely before discovering that he does not mean by these expressions what the Apostles meant, or what the Church has meant. In the strict sense Law was a legalist, but he is saved by his singularly firm hold of the truth that all life in the creature must come from the birth of the holy nature of God. No one insisted more than he did on the sublimity of what the Christian life may be and ought to be, and on the supernatural powers that are available for reaching that height. An extremely able, but as I venture to think not too scrupulous, controversialist, Law never hesitated, never admitted himself to be in the wrong, and treated all differences not indeed with personal acrimony, but with a cold disdain.

Nevertheless it cannot be doubted by any one who looks into the subject that if Wesley had continued to be a disciple of William Law the evangelical revival, so far as it depended on Wesley, would never have existed. When Wesley broke from Law he struck on the way of salvation. It was Peter Böhler who led Wesley into the truth. "Herein is a mystery, here the wise men of the world are lost. Let Thy blood be a propitiation for me." Ever after when Wesley talked of the doctrine of the satisfaction of Christ, he spoke of it as an inmost mystery of the faith. Christ loved His own body less than His mystical body the Church, and therefore gave the former for the latter. Wesley never admitted, and we must never admit, that the doctrine of satisfaction can be made perfectly accessible to the human reason. St. Paul leads us not into the regions of common sense, but into those of profound and awful mystery. Only it is to be maintained that by actual spiritual trial we may know the doctrine and prove it, and live by it, and experience the blessing of justification. We may understand how the Church lives in the strength of her one perpetual oblation and sacrifice, and why the awful Apocalyptic voices do not cease to cry, "Worthy is the Lamb that was slain." The spirit in which Wesley contemplated the great life-giving truth is expressed in his own quotation from Madame Schurmann's pamphlet: "It is precious to those who feel the weight of their sins, who know that they are by nature children of wrath, and at the same time utterly incapable either of paying the debt or rising from the death of sins, of conquering themselves, the world, and the devil, or meriting eternal life."

Yet Law's views have commended themselves from opposite sides to well-accredited evangelical divines. Dr. Whyte, on his side, has done the Church lasting service by his profound consciousness of sin, by the keenness with which he recognises the frailty that clings to even the best works of man, by the sharpness with which he realises the sense of personal guilt. Law's teaching about human nature and about the divine requirement has taken hold of him, and greatly reinforced a tendency that already existed. We need such preaching, and we never needed it more than at a time when the corruption of human nature is preached not so much by believing men as by great unbelieving teachers like Ibsen. Many of us have fallen into the Romish error of thinking, if we do not dare to say, that the corruption of human nature is monstrously exaggerated—a doctrine from which the idea of supererogation naturally springs. But there is a danger in the truer view. It is the danger of forgetting in the torturing consciousness of sin the true and everlasting distinction between those who are justified and those who are not justified. If justification and pardon are confounded, Christians will come to believe that when pardon needs renewal, justification needs renewal also. They will come to think that they are in as unsheltered and perilous a state as they were before reconciliation. The end will be a dejection and weariness of the soul utterly foreign to the buoyancy and triumph of the Apostles, a shrinking from the great language which it becomes the redeemed of the Lord to use. It is true that in all things we offend and come short, but it is true also that to those who believe in Jesus there is granted a great and permanent blessing that cannot be touched by the infirmities, follies and sins which are daily confessed and daily need forgiveness. Justification is reduced to insignificance and worthlessness if day by day we can be thrown back into the wretchedness of being under the divine condemnation.

No preaching can be fully evangelical which does not recognise in every part the infinite significance of this separation. Dr. Dale said with much truth that the great secret of Mr. Spurgeon's power was that he was always fully conscious of his own free justification before God. There are those before the preacher who in Christ are justified. They are to be called to sanctification. There are those who are not justified, and they are to be told that they cannot sanctify themselves, and that their first step is to enter by faith into the condition in which they are accepted in the Beloved as righteous, in which they enter into what is rather unity than union with Christ, in which all the sanctifying forces of the Holy Ghost work upon their souls. And it has to be continually realised that in the Christian experience the sense of personal guilt and the sense of personal deliverance ought not to be severed. If there is no sense of personal guilt, the experience will be at the very best superficial, and if there is no sense of personal deliverance, the experience will be one of groaning and burden, an experience in which the soul is an exile from the joy of our Lord.

On the other hand, Mr. Murray is attracted by Law's call to perfection, and his high standard of Christian holiness. Of Mr. Murray's teaching generally I have no right to speak, but he is more or less identified in the public mind with the school of teachers who proclaim that a higher Christian life is accessible. He mistakes in the most amazing way the ground of Wesley's severance from Law. These theologians for the most part make comparatively little of the satisfaction of Christ to the divine justice, though some of them honestly accept it. They get rid of the sense of guilt. They do not seem to have much or anything to confess. They have doubtless done great service in showing that Christians are prone to rest satisfied with a lower degree of attainment and joy than that which Christ has made possible. That we should ceaselessly aspire to be altogether hopeful, altogether loving, altogether believing, altogether Christian—that is the will of God. And it is right to acknowledge that the Scriptures plainly teach us that experiences which many of us have never shared are possible to the soul that trusts in Christ. We must not make too much of sin or allow it to obscure the effects of grace. We must not deny that great victories have been won by the Spirit of God in human souls. Who can forget the tenderness, the triumph, the quick hope with which the Holy Ghost through the mouth of His servants welcomes every victory over evil? But there are grave dangers of forgetting that we cannot atone either by sorrow or by righteousness, that it is on the finished work of Christ, and on that alone, that we must rely. These teachers so far as I know, like Law, insist on the fact that all Christian graces are the fruits of the Spirit of Christ, but even though they are, they no more avail for salvation than if they were not. It is possible to dwell on these graces until we actually rest upon them for our salvation and seem to lose the very need of pardon. As to whether perfection may be attained in this life it is not necessary to dogmatise. Doubtless the Divine Spirit may subdue and ennoble our disordered natures beyond what may easily be deemed possible. It is a question of experience, and it may be that many of us are of opinion after years and years of communion with them that certain human beings have attained perfection, the perfection that reveals the quality and power of a life that is higher than the earthly. But even if it is so, how could those spirits claim to be perfect? If they were perfect they would be perfect in a kind, pure, self-forgetfulness that would not know its perfection. Such people as I have spoken of are quite unconscious of the goodness of which they are the temples. As to those who profess to be perfect, it is but just to say that they usually make the claim with faltering lips. But has the claim ever been allowed? Is the type of character formed at perfection meetings even up to the ordinary standard of the Christian character? Is it not rather the type of a Christianity which has returned to pietism? And the pietistic morality is piety. Morality in the pietistic view is the sanctification of the individual. In this form of religion the real problem is not dealt with. Pietism does not face life and conquer it, and throw the many-chambered mansions of the soul into one. Resting upon its own achievement it becomes a kind of Christian endæmonism.

In short, one error is common to both schools. They look within and not without—one on indwelling sin and the other on indwelling righteousness. To say that Christ came merely to reveal a higher morality is to be outside of Christianity. For then He would have come to thrust the world into a deeper condemnation. But, blessed be His name, He came not to condemn the world, but that the world, through Him, might be saved. I know no Christian teacher who maintains that Christianity is a system of ethics. But many forget that, when He declared His saving purpose, He went on, and that in the very budding and beginning of His career, to explain how it was to be effected. "As Moses lifted up the serpent in the wilderness, even so must the Son of Man be lifted up, that whosoever believeth in Him should not perish, but have everlasting life." "It is not in our own wounds," says Vinet, "but in the wounds of Jesus that we must put our hands." And for us there is no merit but the merit of His atoning sacrifice.

IV

Much has been necessarily omitted in this brief survey, but enough perhaps has been said to show that in a genuine and normal Christian experience the elements described by Bunyan are still present as much as ever. There is first of all justification by faith by reliance on the finished work of Christ. We have in St. Paul's doctrine not merely a testimony against human merit and self-righteousness. We have not only the true ground but the true mode of our justification by faith—a faith which works by love. As to the ground there is no time to notice the controversy raised among evangelicals as to the active and passive obedience of Christ. Writing against O'Brien, Birks said that Christ was not a substitute in His active obedience to the law of God. That obedience was a privilege and not an evil or a burden, and to be set free from obedience would be a curse and no blessing. Perhaps it would be better to say that all Christ's obedience on earth was an action and a passion. Anyhow, it is upon a work outside of ourselves and unaffected by the fluctuation of our moods that our justification depends. This is a truth which ought to have more place in Christian experience, and I know no more powerful exposition of it than in Dora Greenwell's " Colloquia Crucis." She delights in all statements, however naked and literal, that bring the judicial aspect of

Christ's work into full relief. At the very centre of Christianity in her view lie the doctrines of intervention and substitution. They are the glorious alphabet of Christianity. They may be stammered over, travestied, and vulgarised as by children in a village school, and yet they contain within them all poetry, all eloquence, in their sublimest and tenderest range. We are to take our deliverance as a settled axiom of the soul, as a certainty which remains valid whether we for the moment realise it or not. The Cross and faith in the work wrought upon the Cross is a root that can spring out of a dry ground. "Show Thy servants Thy *work*" is among the deepest of prayers.

And the next element of Christian experience is joy in the Holy Ghost. When the heart truly joins itself to Christ's great sacrifice and to Christ Himself, it can dare and endure all things. It becomes strong, free, untrammelled, unperturbed. It lays hold upon Christ in the fulness of His self-communicating grace. It enters into the kingdom of righteousness and peace and joy in the Holy Ghost. But it does not depend even then on the rise and fall of ecstatic feeling. If the divine act of justification is the bestowal of ecstasy the very foundation of justification is shaken, and growth in sanctification ceases. The true doctrine is that through the gate of God, the Meritorious Sacrifice, the soul enters into the great and comforting reality of pardon and acceptance, into the love and peace and joy of believing, and the Holy Ghost is made to it the Lord and Giver of Life. By Him it subdues kingdoms, works righteousness, obtains promises. By Him it knits and binds together the every day and the everlasting. Nevertheless, it has its sorrows, its failures, its crucifixions, its forsakings, its despairs.

For there is present evermore that aching sense of shortcoming. If we consent to the presence of sin without striving, without repentance, without grief, or if we lower the standard of perfection till it is within our reach, we are guilty of errors which have the same root and the same fruit. Nevertheless, the normal Christian life is the simultaneous presence in the soul of grace and peace, and of the consciousness of sin; and by virtue of our union with Christ we who are still sinners are nevertheless justified, and partakers of the peace of God. So we utterly contemn, slight, and abhor our own righteousness. We slight it as a possible ground of justification before God. We slight it for what it is in itself. Our best achievement is nothing in the face of the eternal throne—so stained is it, so faultful, so sinful in every part. If He will but draw the red line of His blood through the hopeless reckoning of our life! And so it comes that at death believers ever gaze towards the Cross, not to the Crown. The word they need is, "I will be merciful to their unrighteousness and to their righteousness, and their sins and their iniquities will I remember no more." It is difficult in a time like this, which takes the fact of salvation so easily, to understand how hard the first Christians found it to believe, and how strong was the consolation which God administered them. Remember how the Apostle assured his trembling hearers of the awful, incredible wonder of the great salvation. "Wherefore God, willing more abundantly to show unto the heirs of promise the immutability of His counsel, confirmed it by an oath, that by two immutable things in which it was impossible for God to lie we might have a strong consolation who have fled for refuge to lay hold upon the hope set before us." "I die," said one of your own ministers, "resting on oaths and covenants and blood." He utterly abhorred, slighted, and contemned his own righteousness. Over the grave where the body of William Carey waits the Redeemer's return are the words so dear to our fathers—

> "A guilty, weak, and helpless worm
>   On Thy kind arms I fall;
> Be Thou my strength and righteousness,
>   My Jesus and my all."

FROM THE TABERNACLE TO THE HOUSE

WE have written of the normal Christian experience on earth, the experience of faith and joy, of tender contrition, of ardent striving, the experience described by Coleridge as "faith in the God-Manhood, the Cross, the mediation, the perfect righteousness of Jesus to the utter rejection and abjuration of all righteousness of our own." It may reasonably be asked whether this experience will end when the spirit quits its dwelling of clay, and passes, as St. Paul says, from the Tabernacle to the House. "We know that if the earthly house of our tabernacle be dissolved we have a building from God, a house not made with hands, eternal in the heavens. For verily in this we groan, longing to be clothed upon with our habitation which is from heaven, if so be that being clothed we shall not be found naked. For, indeed, we that are in this tabernacle do groan, being burdened, not that we would be unclothed, but that we would be clothed upon, that what is mortal may be swallowed up of life." When the hour comes when we pass at last from the Tabernacle to the House, do we leave sin for ever behind us?

There is no question which up till recently would have been answered in the affirmative with more confidence than this. There is no revelation to which the human heart utters its Amen more surely than to the words, "Blessed are the dead which die in the Lord." Carlyle's strange echo will be remembered among many others, and yet we have seen lately signs of a certain uneasiness. It is asked whether a natural process like death can make such a change. Revolutions in the spiritual life are discredited, and with many the new birth and the birth of the soul into heaven, with its accompanying transformation, are viewed with equal suspicion. The time has come when the doctrine of Scripture and of all Protestant churches on this head needs to be pressed forward by Christian teachers with less reserve, and with more of edge in their language.

It is well to say in the first place that the alternative to this doctrine is the doctrine of Purgatory. The Roman Catholic Church has been singularly cautious in its authoritative declarations on this theme. There are but two, and they tell simply that the truly penitent who have departed this life in the love of God before they have made satisfaction for their sins by fruits meet for repentance, are cleansed by purgatorial pains after death, and may be helped by the suffrages of the living. Of course, popular teaching has been more detailed and explicit, particularly in its disposition to assert the use of literal fire as the cleansing element. But Roman Catholics are not obliged to believe this. What they have to believe in is that Christian souls with sin upon them pass into a state of expiatory suffering, in which they can be helped by the good works of living believers. Now the moment we admit that souls are not perfectly cleansed at death, and that the process of purification goes on in the other life, we are compelled, not indeed to postulate the efficacy of prayers, and alms, and sacrifices on the part of the living, but the existence of an intermediate state from which penitent and sinful souls gradually rise to the world of holiness.

We are also compelled to believe that their purification is, partly at least, accompanied by pain; for so long as sin is present pain must be present also, and under the conditions supposed it must be working for remedial ends. Nor are we able to put any limit on the duration of this period. The arguments which go to show that death does not mark the end of sin go equally to show that the Second Advent does not make an end of sin. Nor have we any clue to guide us to what period may be necessary for many souls in order to free them from their defilement. Protestant theologians naturally shrink from reviving a doctrine not to be found in Scripture, a doctrine which the Reformed Churches entirely reject as the seat of the very worst corruptions. But they cannot logically escape from such conclusion of their argument.

In one of her earliest books, "A Present Heaven," Dora Greenwell urged that there was no such difference between the experience of deliverance in this life and in the other as it was common to suppose. She said that Christians did not sufficiently use and prize the high possibilities of their present state. They were in danger of looking for another Christ than the all-sufficient Saviour already born into the world. More, they were in danger of taking the key from the shoulders of the true Eliakim, who openeth and no man shutteth, when they looked to death as their saviour and deliverer. A mere physical process like that of death could not do the work of faith. There is no theological writer from whom we should dissent more reluctantly and with more unfeigned diffidence than from Dora Greenwell, and much of her teaching in that volume has long perplexed us. It was a great relief the other day to discover a new edition of the book which she had called "The Covenant of Life and Peace," and in which she frankly confesses that she was mistaken, that she had failed to see that the glory of the Celestial is one and the glory of the Terrestrial is another, and that the experiences of the world after death must of necessity be immeasurably higher and greater than in this world of sin and struggle and conflict. True, even here we are reconciled to God by the death of His Son. For us there exists no more the enmity which Christ slew in dying. We are freely justified by His grace, and loosed from our sins in His own blood, and made a kingdom of priests to God, even the Father. Nevertheless, there is before us a grander emancipation, a completer joy, even to love as we are loved, and to know as we are known, to arrive at that full comprehension of Christ which His most favoured servants confess they must still reach after here.

For, to begin with, in dying we pass from the Tabernacle to the House. From the rent and harried home in which we groan, being burdened, from the terrible realisation of what dissolution of soul and body means, from the tent that is ever at the mercy of the circumstances and storms of time, from the weight of care and suffering the body brings, and brings the longer it is inhabited, we pass to the House in the heavens which is God's work and God's gift, and in which we groan no more. It is not in the least necessary in this connection to discuss the question whether St. Paul thought the seat of evil was to be found in the body, nor is it even necessary to discuss the precise interpretation of the passage on which these remarks are based. Even if we concede that the proper translation is, " For this cause we groan "—and the rendering seems to us highly improbable—no student of St. Paul, we had almost said no one who knows what bodily frailty means, could doubt that it was true that St. Paul knew what it is to live in a tent like this, that he understood the humiliation of the body, that sighs and groans were often pressed from him by the load under which he laboured. He had his own dread about death. Of the life to come he never doubted as we do; he had no fear that men eat and drink, and die and vanish like bubbles from the surface of the stream. What he feared was the forlorn wandering of the unhoused spirit. He earnestly desired to be clothed upon with his house from heaven, if so be that being clothed he might not be found naked. As the end came the fear passed away, and it now figures little in Christian experience.

> "Jesus, to Thy dear faithful hand
> My *naked* soul I trust,"

is the word often repeated with great peace at the supreme hour. "I saw the souls of them which had been slain for the Word of God, and there was given them, to each one, a white robe." St. Paul was always at close quarters with death, and he must have judged long before the last that he had to pass through its searching trial. His comfort was that he passed from the Tabernacle to the House.

But the main assurance of perfection at death is the vision of Christ. All dark symbols are for ever done with. We shall see Him as He is, and we shall be like Him. Disclosures incomparably more vivid and more potent than we have ever dreamed of will be granted us when the earthly house of this Tabernacle is dissolved. The soul will be encircled and absorbed in the consciousness of God. "With Christ" is the one piercing word that tears clear the whole clouded heaven to the Apostle—"With Christ which is very far better." Who shall tell what is covered by the word "very far"? Whatever it is, it is enough. "With great mercies will I gather thee," is the divine sentence whispered to the soul. A spiritual operation, it is said, demands a spiritual energy. Yes, but this spiritual energy is exerted on certain conditions, and these conditions are realised in dying. There is then the entire union of the human and the divine. For our part, we take no interest in the speculations as to the *rationale* of this transformation. We may say with Delitzsch that the sanctifying power of faith bursts forth at death, and that the sight of the reality of what is believed will wipe out all sin. We may add with Phillippi that a creative, miraculous act of God always coincides in the death of true believers. But the air is too rarefied. It is wise rather to raise our thoughts to the few illuminated points in the mysterious region, the suns and planets which light up the darkness, and for the rest to lean upon God, and look with calmness into the mysteries which He still leaves so deep around us. These untravelled worlds are more immediately than this within the region of God's rule, and we shall find within them when the time comes the fulness of content.

Once more, it is to be remembered that death lifts the soul into sunshine. It immeasurably extends and glorifies the outward conditions under which the development of life will proceed. We shall find ourselves where not only the first fruits are holy, but where the lump also is holy. We shall be in the fellowship of happy spirits for ever joyful, for ever victorious, for ever conscious of the mighty efficacies of the Christian redemption. Love reaching its climax will cast out fear. Souls perfectly redeemed will drink of the river of God's pleasures and be satisfied. In the full sense then we shall be delivered from this present evil world and translated into the kingdom of God's dear Son.

This perfect life is a life which moves from strength to strength, and which reaches its consummation in the resurrection of the body. Christian apologists have laid too little stress on St. Paul's doctrine of the resurrection of the spiritual body that rises from the corruptible seed. The human wisdom of the ancient world would naturally have taken a view of this which science could not accept. As Christ carried to heaven not a fragment only of our nature, but human nature complete in all the powers that are not essentially connected with mortality, so His people are clothed at last in a new body through which the soul speaks. "A body hast Thou prepared me," is the faith and hope of the blessed dead. One recalls Isaac Taylor's quaint and suggestive interpretation of St. Paul's words before Agrippa about the promise of the resurrection unto which the twelve tribes instantly serving God day and night hope to come. He refers it to the tribes who have gone up thither, who have every one of them appeared in Sion and before God. He takes the worship of the desert as a symbolic model of the invisible economy of spirits, of the state into which the few brief years of mortal life are to bring every true worshipper.

In the furthest recess of the sacred pavilion is displayed the visible splendour of the Divine Presence. Before the Shekinah are the cherubs symbolising the constant adoration of the angels; the tokens of the mediatorial covenant rest at the foot of the throne. The mediator intercedes within the inner chamber, and without the veils are seen the seven lamps. From without the veil goes up the perpetual incense of prayer from the assembled thousands of Israel devoutly expecting. The promise of the blessed resurrection, never made in fulness to the Israelites before Christ, is conveyed to them on their entrance upon the world of souls, and there they, not having received the promise, but waiting through the distant lapse of ages, keep Sabbath with the people of God till He whose memorial is with them rises suddenly from His throne within the veil, and comes forth to accomplish the redemption of the body.

THE VALUE OF PECULIAR POSSESSIONS[*]

NOT far from the heart of a great modern city, you will sometimes come across old walls and gateways which have been outgrown. What was once country is now suburb, and what was once suburb is now city. The venerable landmarks remain, but the true boundary continually stretches itself further out. This should be a picture of your life if you continue to the end students of divinity. You will fail if what now marks the limit of your attainment and thought is not transcended. But you will equally fail if what you possess now does not remain to the end central. If it is overthrown and dishonoured, there is a real danger that no soul city will ever take its place. What this college should do for

[*] Address delivered at the close of the Session in Hackney Theological College, June 16, 1896.

you is to enclose you in a small circle permanent at the centre, but ever tending to widen at the circumference. A small circle it must be, for all you know now of God and of the things of God cannot be much. Yet if the centre is fixed, it is that from which future thought and knowledge radiate, and you will constantly go back to it in the end, however free and spacious and fair your life may grow.

I wish to speak of the value of things which are your very own, of which you may make yourselves masters, and by possession of which you may gain an enduring influence in the kingdom of God. Much, very much, you must of necessity have in common with others, but your lives will make no mark if in addition there is not something which is your peculiar possession.

I

In the first place you must find your own field of reading. It is not uncommon, in speaking to divinity students, to disparage reading. They are warned against it as the idlest of human occupations. And no doubt it is quite as important to say, Think, think, think, as to say, Read, read, read. It is true that the greatest men of all time have read extremely little. You will remember how it was said of Descartes, for example, that he cared very little for reading, and that he left behind him an exceedingly small collection of books. But when one comes to think of it, is it true that people are so very much addicted to reading? How many men of your acquaintance are there who would gladly forego almost any engagement for the sake of a few hours' quiet reading? Is it not so that the vast majority read only if they can find nothing else to do? How many ministers are there who have a passion for reading? It is perhaps not fair to appeal to the size of their libraries, for the owners are as a rule poor, and have not many opportunities of getting books. Yet in this, too, the adage holds that where there is a will there is a way. In the course of my life I do not think I have met with half a dozen persons whose reading could be said to be very wide or various. Further, of these there was not one who had not greatly benefited by his reading, and was not enabled through his knowledge of books to exercise an influence which he would not otherwise have possessed. I am looking in vain for two persons whom one frequently hears denounced in sermons and in addresses—the man who wastes his time in omnivorous reading, and the Christian who needs to be warned against expecting too much in the way of answer to prayer. But passing from this point, you ought to find the line of reading that is congenial to you, and to master in some measure one corner at least of the great realm of knowledge. There is no kind of reading that people so much delight in as lists of books recommended by experts. The recommendations are never perhaps carried out, but there is a glow of virtue and hope in perusing them which has an endless fascination. Remember that there is a limit to the usefulness of such lists. I have read a new book by an eminent Wesleyan minister which is extremely typical. If you turn over it you find references to the books which, as we are told, everybody should read in these days, and which as a matter of fact many do read—the books of Wendt, and George Adam Smith, and Drummond, and Gore, and the rest. It is certainly well to be abreast of current literature, but the best literature is not current, and reading of that kind inevitably issues in what is commonplace and superficial. Let me suggest some lines along which reading may be accomplished.

A deep and thorough familiarity with the text of the English Bible is a rare and precious attainment. To have one copy in large type in which you mark passages and make annotations for a lifetime, which you peruse and re-peruse by day and by night is an enriching thing. It was said of Dr. Emmons, the New England divine, who had few books, that he read and re-read the English Bible so often and so carefully that its words came to him like nimble servitors and stood waiting for his call. In religious books like these of Henry Dunn—books which owe very little to general reading or to intellectual power or genius—you will often find a phrase that charms by its grace, but is hidden like the trailing arbutus among the leaves of a preceding summer, and as you inspect the phrase more narrowly you find it a choice but concealed quotation. This refinement and distinction of expression often characterises the prayers of humble believers who know but one book. Another line of reading extremely profitable, but much neglected, is that of religious biography. It is amazing to find ministers who do not know even such a great storehouse of thought as the "Life of John Foster." Or it may be wise to extend your reading beyond the limits of your own church and country. I venture to say that there is very much to be learned from the great French Roman Catholic writers like Ozanam, Lacordaire, De Maistre, Père Gratry, and others. It was from these that Dora Greenwell mainly derived in her profound theological essays, and the influence which has been exerted by Gratry over the younger school of High Churchmen in this country is the more amazing the more it is investigated. Perhaps you may be able to add something to the literature of devotion or theology, and how many obvious blanks there are in this field. For example, I do not know in the English language a single great or complete book on prayer, a book dealing frankly with the teaching of Scripture. Nor do I know any work in which the significance of forgiveness is at all adequately discussed. The way in which forgiveness comes is one of the great topics of theology, but it is equally important to understand what forgiveness means. In any case you may rest assured that there is no danger and no temptation you need fear less than the danger of reading too much. Lagarde said in his bitter, piercing way, "*Theologorum eos mores esse scimus ut libros scribant multi, legant pauci, emant nulli.*" "We know that those are the ways of theologians, that many write books, few read them, and none buy them."

II

I pass on to say something of opinions. Your opinions to be of true avail must be your very own. In these days of controversy many people seem to make up their minds by striking an average between the extremes represented by various champions. They like to be called moderate men, and are great in condemning "the falsehood of extremes." But they never look at any question directly with their own eyes. That is too anxious a task. But they think they are likely to be near the mark if they stand in the middle. For example, the higher criticism is up for discussion. These persons read that some scholars maintain that Isaiah was written by one man, and others maintain, let us say, that there were three authors. The people of whom I am speaking would shrink from the labour necessary to understand why the Isaianic authorship is disputed, but are probably willing to compromise upon two authors. In the same way, when practical questions which need not be referred to are up, they veer uneasily between opposing hosts, watching day by day how the clamour rises and falls. They sometimes conclude that they can be in both camps at once by saying that one is logical and the other practical. Sir Boyle Roche said that a man could not be in two places at once unless he were a bird. Ecclesiastics are not birds, and even if they were—— The fact is that many questions altogether refuse to be compromised. The *tertium quid* is generally, like a quack medicine, vulgar and impossible, and its meaning is that the right is never on one side and the wrong on another. There was once on a time high debate in a town whether the streets should be watered or not. The controversy waxed furious. The anti-water party hated the slop of watered roads, and maintained generally that the watering was a useless expense and a waste of the water supply. The water party enlarged on the discomfort of the dust, and the injury it caused to goods in shops. The wrangle continued until the mayor, penetrated with the belief that compromises are the very essence of constitutionalism, offered a solution of the difficulty. He proposed that the water-carts should perambulate the streets, but that there should be no water in them. He was held by acclamation to have evinced statesmanlike qualities of the highest order, and the meeting broke up in peace, perfectly satisfied that a good result had been achieved. It is not your business to be in a majority. It may be your duty all your life to buffet a strong current in Church and State. There are Three that bear record in heaven, and if your witness goes with theirs, the rest do not count at all.

III

But I wish to speak mainly of the necessity of having, as your very own, religious convictions. There is no kind of criticism you are to encounter which will puzzle you half so much as that of humble exercised believers who are not edified by your preaching. You may take a very modest view of your own sermons, and willingly accept suggestions from those you recognise as your intellectual equals or superiors. But you will learn, perhaps slowly and painfully, that the true arbiters are those who have been taught of the Holy Ghost and who find in Christ their all. They may not be able to put into words the knowledge they have won, but they can judge very well whether in the substance of your ministry you are faithful to revelation. Let us trace the law of the great decisive disclosures. It is a familiar truth that grief is a great teacher. Not till we have looked with yearning agony into these last things beyond the veil are we able to understand the enduring books of sorrow. It is hardly possible, for example, that a young man can in the full sense appreciate Tennyson's "In Memoriam," and you will find in Dr. Hort's recently published "Life" how he grew in his estimation of the poem. Life and experience are interpreters in the lower plane, but in the region where you must move freely there is no interpretation save that of the Holy Ghost. Learning in a Christian minister is a desirable possession; eloquence is a rare and noble gift; the power of brilliant, pungent, memorable writing is much to be coveted; a familiarity with contemporary thought puts you in easy relation with the minds of your people. All these things, however, are of subordinate importance, and do not affect the essentials of the Christian ministry. What Christian preachers should be is described by St. Paul. They should be ministers of Christ and stewards of the mysteries of God. Now, it would be cruel and unjust to deny that in a sense most preachers are ministers of Christ. Nearly all preachers believe that our Lord Jesus Christ fulfilled the office of a prophet in His estate of humiliation, and thereby, if not otherwise, acquired a certain shadowy kingship over the quick and dead. But it is not every minister whom you would readily and naturally call a steward of the mysteries of God. The mysteries of God are not, of course, the Christian sacraments. They are the august and awful revelations of Christ, which constitute the wisdom that was hidden, but is now revealed to the Church. They are the truths contained in and proceeding from the facts that Our Lord in His humiliation and His exaltation fulfilled the office of the Prophet, the Priest, and the King of His Church, and that we are the House of Christ, if we hold fast the confidence and the rejoicing of the hope firm unto the end. There is much in the Bible that he who runs may read. There is a natural sense discovered by the grammar and the lexicon. But nothing which the unaided reader is able to discover is of true saving worth. The mysteries of God are revealed only to humble souls on bended knees. In other words, for the understanding of all the great truths which must constitute the strength of the Christian ministry, there must be an immediate and supernatural illumination. There is no need to deny the value of speech. It will do much. There are runes and spellwords by which marvels are wrought in the poet's heaven of invention. But what is needed is that your hearers should feel the shock of a vital battery, and such a battery is neither to be filled nor discharged by words. No learning and no power of intellect can by itself increase the substance of your knowledge of divine and eternal truths. And those who possess no learning, but who have studied the mind of the Spirit, those in whom Christ survives, are able to judge you and your sermons, to recognise the field which the Lord hath blessed and the streams that make glad the tabernacles of the Most High. I believe that no power of vision avails anything beyond the light contained in the page of revelation. But it is not wonderful when merely intellectual preachers become the rulers in the Church that the people turn to anything in the form of spiritual instruction. In the era of corrupt and formalised Lutheranism, when the spirit of the Reformation was lost in the letter, when every one argued about Calvinism and crypto-Calvinism, people turned with baited tempers and barren hearts to the mystic Jacob Böhme. And so it will be again. Many of you perhaps can never be eloquent. You can never achieve fresh discoveries in the intellectual construction of saving truth. But this may be yours if you seek it—a knowledge of the mysteries of God—and it is an endowment so precious that all the rest are not to be named in comparison with it. It is stewards of the mysteries of God, speaking with the accent of the Holy Ghost, that the Church in these days supremely needs. And this knowledge must be in a very peculiar sense your own. No man, no book can impart it to you. It must be learned direct from God Himself.

I believe that for the most part a faithful ministry of Christ will not lack encouragement, even outward encouragement. And yet there are cases where one is baffled to understand the secret of failure. Still, to the faithful there is no failure. I recall a beautiful comparison suggested by Alfred Vaughan. Many a sunset has seemed a vain splendour, burning itself away in the west down to the water's edge. When its fires are spent a sombre chill falls over all things. But these very vapours, gorgeous with such blazonry, are drawn through the cooling air. They creep along the fields, and hang their multitude of drops upon the dusty bushes and the shrunken flowers. It may come to pass that some of these very drops, coloured a short while since with such a red fire in the heart of the sky, shall live transformed a crimson life again in the red petals of the rose, and that the golden overlaying of the heavens will take substance and reappear as the dust in the heart of some flower that completes its beauty with the clammy moisture. These emblems of fancy show forth the realities of faith, and represent that law of love which suffers no true words and no holy endeavours utterly to perish, even when to mortal eyes they are lost and dead. Nothing in what I have said is to be taken in disparagement of intellectual culture. But you must be able to say, "I have made my heart a holy sepulchre, and all my land of thought a Palestine." And it is not by learning or talent, but by keeping the springs of your life full, that you will be upborne through weariness and care and sorrow and conflict, and enabled to endure to the end, and counted at last worthy to attain that world and the resurrection from the dead.

THE LONG LOVE OF CHRIST

THE stronghold of the biblical doctrine of election is to be found in Our Lord's words. Stated in dogmatic form, this great truth has lost its hold on the consciousness of the Church, and almost everywhere has disappeared into the background. Yet the time must come when it will resume its old place. We cannot afford to be ignorant that God " did not wait to love us till this late, lonely moment which we call our life, that these poor years are steeped in the light of everlasting years." The regions of the spirit are but little to be measured by the standards of time, and the thought that God loved us when we did not love Him is infinitely precious. His love was before our knowledge, before our being. It knew all, was mindful of all, embraced its children even in their sleep, even in their dreams, unlighted by any thought of it. Often in this world two come together after each has lived a lifetime. Each finds in the other what the heart has been seeking all the while through lonely, uncomforted years. There is nothing to mar the gladness of that great discovery, save the one thought that each has missed so much of the other's experience, and now the journey is short. It is not so with the eternal, inalienable love of Christ. The eternity of redeeming love expresses itself in experience as security. When we look at Our Lord's last words to the disciples and to the Father, it is plain that the eternal choice to His mind is the assurance that His people are safe. God gave Christ power over all flesh that He should give eternal life to as many as the Father had given Him. The men whom God gave Christ out of the world were God's, and God gave them to Christ. For these He prayed, for they were God's and His. His human consciousness might almost have reeled under the thought of all they had to pass through, when His visible presence was no longer with them. Nevertheless the purpose of God must stand. They were so few and so feeble—their foes were so many, so strong, so unrelenting, that it seemed inevitable they should be swept away by the tide of hate. They were to be condemned, persecuted, slain, and all in the name of God. But the love of the Father who gave them in answer to the love of Christ would not fail. And their Redeemer willed that they should be with Him where He was, that they should behold His glory, and that will of His would triumph, no matter what withstood it. The sheep of Christ should never perish, neither should any pluck them out of His hand. Can we afford to miss the knowledge of divine pledges, divine care, divine purpose in such a world as this which surrounds us, amid so many deadly antagonists of love? If the keeping of the love of Christ depended on ourselves, our heart's best treasure would be insecure. But if He has loved us from before the foundation of the world, who shall separate us from the love of Christ?

The long love of Christ, stretching from eternity to eternity, had its special time of manifestation and appeal. When we were blind and deaf and dumb to Love, Love called us from Calvary. Christ became incarnate, and for our sakes made the journey from "the poor manger to the bitter cross." He came into the world not as a shoot from the innermost pith of divinely endowed human nature, for that nature was diseased, but as a root out of a dry ground, as the Word made flesh. As He hung on Calvary in His mortal wounds, He disclosed Love's very heart. When men in their hardness desired to know nothing of Love, Love refused to forsake them, Love had compassion upon them, and manifested Itself anew to them in the work of redemption. We know how it is with human affection. It becomes as the years pass tranquil and for the most part silent. It is content with the memory of its old sweet time of speech. How often between two who have taken the long path together, the divine words rise in the heart, though they may be unspoken: "I remember thee, the kindness of thy youth, the love of thine espousals when thou wentest after me in the wilderness in a land that was not sown." "When thou wentest after me in a land not sown"—that is, when you went with me into the backwoods, into the bush, when you were so brave and faithful, when your spirit rose superior to all our straits and toil, when you heartened me as I was sinking, when you made our poor pittance go so far, when the glory of your love transfigured the hard and poverty-stricken days. When such memories rise in a husband's heart, everything else is forgotten. The work of time and toil is undone. More than the long vanished loveliness shines from the worn features—they are illuminated in the light of the heart of God. And so the long love of Christ has spoken to us once and for ever from the cross on which He died, and in the light of it we perceive in all our history, in nature, and in providence what Heinrich Müller has finely called "the preaching love of God."

All human love, the noblest, the purest, the tenderest, has its strange alternations, its terrible checks and pauses. But to the communication of the long love of Christ there need be no end. We are able to think of that Love without the shadow of fear. In how many homes love and pain are joined together! And the one makes the other grow. Though the love is perfect and unclouded in itself, although almost impregnable fortresses have been built against worldly care, the shadow of death begins to fall, and there is never a moment of true peace. Charlotte Brontë wrote about her dying sister Emily: "I cherish hope as well as I can, but her appearance and her symptoms tend to crush that feeling. Yet I argue that the present emaciation, cough, weakness, shortness of breath, are the results of inflammation now, I trust, subsided, and that with time these ailments will gradually leave her. But my father shakes his head and speaks of others of our family once similarly afflicted, for whom he likewise persisted in hoping against hope, and who are now removed where hope and fear fluctuate no more. There were, however, differences between their case and hers, important differences I think. I must cling to the expectation of her recovery. I cannot renounce it." But the blow fell, as it falls so often, and what then? Even when we have received to the full all divine consolation, even when we have submitted ourselves completely to the truth and will of God, the fact remains that the great separation has now taken place, and that we miss the daily, hourly assurance of affection which was once our life. We may say with full hearts, " Even so, Father." We may perfectly realise that the vision of the beloved, if it were again bestowed, would smite us to the earth as dead. We may know that any meeting of the earthly consciousness with the exalted spirit would almost break down the powers of the mind and of life. Yet still we are not content.

> "Could I but win thee for one hour from off that starry shore,
> The hunger of my heart were stilled for death hath told thee more
> Than the melancholy world doth know, things deeper than all lore."

But in place of the earthly affection, lost in some measure for the time, we have the constant presence of the love of Christ, a presence which, if we will, is always seeking to break into communication and comfort and strength. The expression of love is not giving, not sacrifice, but love, and the long love of Christ is ever waiting to be gracious. As St. Augustine has said, "the divine love is a *caressing* love." This is the true Easter message, the message of the eternal presence of the risen Saviour.

The long love of Christ, as it began in eternity, stretches on through eternity. Indeed, it is this that makes the thought of eternity bearable. For all things are mortal saving only love. All things, however sweet, however prized, will at length begin to fail, and when the time comes we shall be glad of their failure. But who that has loved has ever desired an end to love? Who that has loved has ever felt the interruption of love as anything but the chief calamity of life, a cruel break in the eternal and divine order, the bitterest penalty of wrong-doing? The love which is so near us, and in which our earthly life may be spent in all its labour and conflict, is the love that stretches out to the endless end. Those who have gazed already, as spirits may gaze, on the face of the eternal Christ, have found it in its perfected manifestation, and we go forward to meet them. To the heavenly Jerusalem, the city of peace, the redeemed of the Lord go up from all the lands of life. And if we are Christ's, received into the communion of the Redeemer and His righteousness, we shall feel that this and this only is our true home, and we shall draw near to it, not timidly, not shrinkingly, but with eager desire, as those who are no more strangers and foreigners, but fellow-citizens with the saints and of the household of God. As we understand the depth of the final rest, we grow reconciled to our bereavements. It seems indeed more natural that the beloved should be withdrawn from us than that they should ever have been at our side.

Our Easter message then is that all of us may find, and find now and find never again to lose, the present love of Christ. How many in weary and craving solitude through dark and melancholy years have been seeking the crown that has never come! They have been saying,

> "Does Love descend from heaven like light,
>   Or grow like flowers out of the ground?
> For I mean to seek him day and night,
>   Till I find him, dear, as you have found."

"Seek what ye seek," says St. Augustine—"it is not where ye seek it." Human nature only feels at home and well and safe and sound in love, but earthly love, at least in full and satisfying measure, may be denied.

"'If I had married Aaron Miles,' went on Aurelia thoughtfully, 'I might have had trials in plenty. I reckon I was bound to, although that's as the Lord wills; I'm not maintaining I shouldn't, but I guess that dreadful sort of useless feeling I never should have known. It's rather unfair I should know it, too, seeing there's plenty of women, and unmarried ones too, that don't have it. I just tried once to explain it to Mehitabel, and I guess you should have seen her stare. I don't rightly know why I'm telling you now, only all this anxiety tells on me. Seems as if I had to talk, or I should die right away. So the years went on at home, and sometimes, although I was always very quiet, the thought of, maybe, all I might have had but for poor Mehitabel's principles, and all the love I had missed, just grew intolerable. It was not the being loved myself I cared for so much as finding folk I could love that I wanted. Why, there have been days when I could hardly bear the sight of a child's face, or the sound of its little, shrill voice, through thinking that had things been different——'"

But love is at our side with its wealth of grace and peace, love in which the soul may find its happiness and the heart its true life. He who lived and died for us, and lives for evermore, is near us all in our loneliness and our lovelessness, and is still saying, "Come unto me, all ye that labour and are heavy laden, and I will give you rest"—rest in love.

THE SORROWS OF THE SAVIOUR

"IT pleased the Lord to bruise Him." He was "acquainted with grief." It had to be so, for the Incarnate Saviour, with His messages and burdens, could not come in the form of a radiant angel, or as one of the bright and gay. But the words carry far more meaning than this. They mean that His experience was solitary, for it has been truly said that we know not what sorrow is, neither are we really acquainted with grief. We have seen the black surface of the Stygian pool and felt the chilling mists that rise from it. But we have not penetrated the abyss or plunged into its drowning waters. Sorrow has been our companion. She has walked for a season by our side in black garments, with veiled face and with a voice of grief. But we have not received her into our flesh and our heart for ever. Our Lord was to be made in the days of His flesh one spirit and one body with grief. For him the veil was lifted from death and hell. In the hand of the Lord there was a cup which He was to taste for us, taste in the sense that He should experience the full bitterness of each drop and be verily acquainted with grief.

It was by degrees that He reached this awful knowledge. From the first it pleased the Lord to bruise Him. He must have experienced the keen pain of a nature wholly pure surrounded by the guilty. When He comes full into our view, we see first His heart of compassion and hope. His heart was touched by the pain of the world. The voice of suffering was heard by Him in every wind of heaven, and rang in His ears till He died. But for suffering He was able to do much. He could speak peace in absolutions and blessing. He could work His wonderful works of love. In the morning watch, in the evening meditation, in the stilling of pain, in the answering of human needs, He carried our sorrows. But as time went on He endured the contradiction of sinners against Himself. His miracles did not work the end He was striving for. Even when the dumb were speaking, when the lame were leaping, when the devils were fleeing, when the dead were rising, His triumph was incomplete. For the world did not believe His report. He was the arm of the Lord revealed to men, and they were blinded. For the sinner's sake He descended into what we call hell. He sought the outcast in her trembling shame. He offered Himself separately to the guilty one by one. With the clearest perception of human suffering there was always combined in Him the consciousness of knowing a great light and a saving name. His speech was not the mere words of a human being, but the breakers of the Everlasting Love itself as they rolled in and shattered themselves on this bank and shoal of time. But He came to His own and His own received Him not. In the name of the law and the prophets they rejected Him in whom the law and the prophets ended and were lost. We can see how His anguish rose at the successive impediments to His godly purpose. We can see how He was moved with an overwhelming fear for the rebellious as the world's enmity disclosed itself to Him. As the months passed and the mystery of iniquity and the devices of Satan became more and more clear, we can understand how He said to Himself,

"Why art Thou as a man ashamed, as a mighty man that cannot save?" He seemed to be striking into the air, preaching and toiling without fruit. Yet in Him faith never staggered. Hope was never eclipsed. Love was never dried up. Of God's fulness He always received, and grace for grace. He acquiesced and rested in the Everlasting Love that foreknew and chose, and would give to Himself the sheep for whom He died; and yet we know how He spake about Chorazin and Bethsaida, where His miracles were done in vain, and how He wept as he saw the eyes of the Jerusalem that slew Him close for ever. And so He saw the cup approaching, the cup which held the sorrow which is more than the sorrow of a rejected messenger, even though the rejected messenger was the Eternal Son.

Next there came what we may call the far-off vision of the supreme sorrow. He had known it from the very beginning. But it grew clearer as He advanced, and He set His face steadfastly to go to Jerusalem. He must suffer many things of the elders and chief priests and scribes, and be killed. The arm of the Lord was made bare in miracle and preaching, in flesh and blood, but it had to be made bare in agony before its work was done. Still, may we not say reverently that the crisis of His pain did not come till the cup was close to His lips? We can ourselves partly understand what it is to bear a sorrow that is deferred. For when it is deferred, we picture to ourselves the light that lies beyond it, and so did He. Through the proclamation of His death there rang the cry of triumph, "And be raised again the third day," and from the distance He could see the glory of the resurrection shining on the Cross. He knew that He could not make a tabernacle with His saints on the mountain, and linger always there. He knew that the ecstasy of the exalted heart must pass with the drifting cloud and with the withdrawing vision. He never deceived Himself, as we do who know not what a day may bring forth. We pretend we do not know, and cheat ourselves with hope. The delusion helps us. We even seem to rise up by degrees to take hold of life for a time. His vision was clearer, and still for Him also day dawned after day, evening after evening closed in, and the dreadful hour was not yet come. But it was coming. It was not far away, and He always knew that through His travail and agony, His cross and wounds, the redemption of the world must be accomplished.

Then came the time when the cup drew nearer and nearer to the paling lips, and when manifestly the last hours and sorrows were nigh. And that was Gethsemane. That was the prayer of prayers: "Father, if it be possible, let this cup pass from me. Nevertheless, not my will, but Thine be done." *Transeat calix*—let this cup pass. That we say is the prayer of prayers. There is no time in which we cry to God as we do when His sword is lifted to smite us, and when yet it seems as if it might be turned aside; when the grief which we have long seen with foreboding tears comes to us, and there are but minutes, or at most hours, when we can plead. Then the deep of misery calls to the deep of mercy, and we know in the full sense what it is to pray *Transeat calix*—let this cup pass. It seems as if everything we could desire and everything we could hope for were summed up in the passing of the cup. Once the cup was not in sight, or dreamt of, and yet oftentimes we fancied that life was grey. But now there is nothing to ask but one thing, and if that one thing were given we feel that we should never ask from

God anything more. Let this cup pass. Let it just but be as it used to be, and we shall be more blessed than we ever were in our wildest dreams. When it looks as if the intensity of our praying might decide the wavering balance, how the heart gathers itself up, how it pours its emotion in full tide, how it seems to greaten and grow irresistible, as if it might even wrestle with God and prevail. This was how Our Lord prayed in Gethsemane. But He prayed as we cannot always pray, with perfect submission. We strive and struggle, we turn this way or that for a door of escape, we would force our wills upon God. But He, when He put His hand to the plough, did not draw back, and never once drove an unsteady furrow, though His prayer was for a greater deliverance than ever was asked for by merely human lips. For at the moment He went down into—was lost and disappeared in—grief, as He disappeared when He was once buried in the waters of baptism. The Lord entered the awful regions spoken of by the Greek Church as His unknown sufferings—τὰ ἄγνωστα παθήματα. The rebuke that broke His heart was the gathered rebukes of all His people, the rebukes that else would have broken their hearts for ever in an irremediable pang. We can never understand the depth of that suffering. Suffice it that an angel came to help Him when He seemed to be swooning into death. The anticipation of great agony, its rehearsal, is often the chief element in the agony. When it is passed the worst is passed, especially if we know that the anguish is to be an end of all anguish, and that death is behind. When once the spirit has sobbed out, "Thy will be done," the rest seems little. As the great heroisms of life are often preceded by inward conflict of which the world knows nothing, but which is far harder than the outward conflict, so the great griefs of life are suffered often in secret ere they come to open manifestation. His warfare in a sense was accomplished at Gethsemane, and thenceforth He strove no more. He was led as a lamb to the slaughter, and as a sheep before her shearers is dumb, so He opened not His mouth.

Last of all there came to Him the sorrow of the Cross, the hours of the open shame and the power of darkness, of the nails, the thorns, the hammer, the bowed head, the death-cry, and the death. It was not all darkness, for, as one of the

Fathers has written, He died in the risen sunshine of God's name, every cloud flying, and the clear sky returning. He knew that when all was over He was to be the chief cornerstone of the Eternal City, never to be moved nor disquieted again. There is a certain dreadlessness in Our Lord's agony, a peace, a serenity, a feeling of a travail gone through and ended, never to return. Yet that we may remember His unknown sufferings, that we may understand that He died as our substitute, and that He was bearing for the sins of His people the weight of the divine wrath, we have the peace broken by the dreadful cry, "My God, my God, why hast Thou forsaken me?" Then we know that He has touched the last depth of the last abyss. And these things were done in the Tree whose root and head was God! It was thus that ☦ Love bore the sin of the world. Then the cup of wrath was laid down, and He took in His hand for ever the cup of blessing. He had gone through what we may reverently call His deep baptism into humanity, whence come those closest interlacings, intercessions, and tenderness of His eternal high priesthood. And all we who are baptized in Christ Jesus are baptized into His death.

"A LISTENER UNTO DEATH"[*]

I WISH to set forth briefly and simply an argument for Christianity, that argument for Christianity which becomes more and more convincing as the years advance. Whatever we may think of Christianity, we are all agreed that it is right to do right, and good to be good. Duty is God's compass to the end of all worlds. That faith remains with us even when we are most beclouded and most in doubt.

Now Christianity is simply a method of goodness. The will of God is our sanctification, and Christianity is His means of effecting that end. Has it effected it? The answer is given in history. Since the day on which Christ died, or rather since the very early morning when He abolished death, there has been in the world the wonderful Church of Christ. Let us for the

[*] Address delivered to the students of Smith College, Northampton, Mass., Sunday, October 11, 1896.

present ignore all distinctions. They are deep, but the unity of the Church is deeper. You know that there are everywhere companies of people all striving after goodness, after truth, after purity, and all of them confessing Christ as Lord. To call upon the name of Christ and to depart from iniquity is to be a member in full communion with the Catholic Church of Jesus Christ. You know this with a nearer intimacy of knowledge. There is not one of you who has not come close to one or more of those who are true witnesses of the Saviour. Our great privilege in this life and our great responsibility is that each of us has known some who through all their innocent years clave to that which is good, lived with absolute unselfishness and unwavering trust. Though they never realised it themselves, and died in unconscious simplicity and humility, it seemed to us who were beside them that they were even in this life without fault before the throne of God, and that they might face without fear that last scrutiny of the Lord. Whatever we may doubt, that remains to us steadfast and unchallenged. And if that remains, everything remains. In days when men make sport of the sweetest certainties, the sweet certainty of the

Christian character abides, and the other certainties are involved and guaranteed by that. For nothing is more sure than that the Christian character is the result of Christianity. It has often been pointed out that its very virtues are a new creation. Take, for example, the virtue of purity. Who will dispute that this virtue was created by Christianity, and that Christianity alone can save it? Remove from the world to-day the companies of confessing believers, and you destroy that fair structure of aspiration and achievement which testifies that Christ has not lived and died in vain. It is idle to dispute this. We see that wherever Christianity is openly and definitely rejected, the Christian law of purity is selected for immediate attack. Beginning at the outworks, the citadel is at last assailed, and mankind is left to sink back into the soil and the beast.

Observe, in the second place, that all these members of Christ unite in ascribing their victory over sin to a power outside themselves. They passionately disclaim any praise of their own effort, their own desire. It was not merely by desiring to be good and striving to be good that they became good. They all of them say *Non nobis*—not unto us. They say that a power from outside nerved the failing forces of their will, guided them, blessed them, redeemed them. If we care to have theological language, we shall hear them all say that they owed everything to the succours of grace. Or if we care to listen to the last and deepest word of Christian experience on earth, and to the new song in heaven, we shall find them saying, in the words whose unimaginable wonder eternity will not exhaust, that they washed their robes and made them white in the blood of the Lamb. But it is unnecessary for our purpose to use theological language at all. Suffice it to say that we have the unbroken company of witnesses, the very flower and crown of earth's virtue and loveliness, saying with one voice, *Non nobis*—not unto us. Can we set aside this testimony? The testimony is that to those who believe in Christ help is given by which they overcome the world.

The argument of Hume against miracles is well known. It is that the experience of mankind is against the occurrence of miracles, and that the testimony for miracles is open to so much doubt that the experience must count for more than the testimony. Certainly, if all miracles ceased when the last of the Apostles died, it will be difficult to meet this reasoning. But our contention is that miracles have never ceased, and that they are still among us in their most amazing form. It was indeed a transcendent experience to live on earth while Christ was yet in the flesh, to see Him lay His hand upon brows burning with fever and make them cool, to hear Him calling into the dull, cold ear of death, and winning answer and obedience. But Our Lord said Himself, "Greater works than these shall ye do," and His word has been fulfilled. The miracle of a renewed heart is matter of our knowledge every day. So then the Church of Christ is the argument for Christianity. Balzac, who, whatever else may be said about him, is assuredly the greatest of Christian novelists, by far the most profound interpreter of that mystery of expiation and redemption which is at the heart of Christianity, has somewhere a picture of the Church of Christ marching side by side with humanity, consoling and sustaining her. What, he asks, if her great companion were to sink down on the road and die, leaving humanity to go on her forlorn and helpless way? Everything would have vanished then which now holds us to duty and to hope.

For those of you who are Christians these considerations have an obvious message. It is from you that others will learn or not learn of Christ and His grace. One of the greatest thoughts that has penetrated English theology in the present generation is that of the Incarnation as hallowing all life. You are to carry Christ into every sphere of your activity. "On His head are many crowns," and you are to crown Him King of your studies. He is the King of kings not the kings of earthly descent merely, but as well the kings of mind and heart. Into literature, into music, into art, into the chosen labour of your mortal years, you are to carry the thought of Christ, and His light is to shine forth from all these. He is indeed to be confessed with the lips. That great duty of confession which is put by St. Paul as the primary condition of salvation never needed more to be enforced than now. But besides that confession of the Lord Jesus with the mouth, and besides that belief in the heart that God hath raised Him from the dead, there is to be also a silent, perpetual acknowledgment of Him hallowing everything you do and say.

You cannot live like this to the end without

hearing and obeying your calls. It was said of Christ Himself that He was obedient unto death—in other words, a listener unto death. From the first to the last Our Lord was listening, always listening, for the still, small voice of God. If you listen, you will hear that voice everywhere. You will hear it especially in those needs of others which are so many perpetual calls. Let us not be deaf to them until it is too late to answer. One of your own novelists has said that in the resurrection we shall all of us first take to confession—confession not to God, but to the brother and sister we have wronged. Our first business will hardly be with God, but with those whom death took from us ere we could obtain from them a forgiveness almost more necessary than God's own. It is vain for us to ask it here.

> " So I hid my face in the grass,
> Whispered, ' Listen to my despair,
> I repent me of all I did.
> Speak a little.' "

But we find no place of repentance, though we seek it carefully with tears. We shall hear His call in nature, which, if our ears are open, will be vocal with remonstrance and appeal. Walking in a wood this afternoon, I thought of Balzac's words on the subduing and mysterious influence of a forest, which he ascribes to the sublime and subtle effect of the presence of so many creatures, all obedient to their destinies, immovable in submission. Christ was always listening to the voice of nature, to the voice of men, to the multitude on whom He had compassion. And God spoke through them to His soul.

And we must be listeners unto death. We most of us hear quickly and well at first. When we are young we see visions and dream dreams, and the high voices fall on us not in vain. But we grow old and deaf and dull. We decline from the lofty, the generous, the unselfish passion that makes youth so beautiful. That it need not be so Our Lord has shown us. He was a listener unto death, and we, like Him, may keep listening through the years of labour, and grief, and disenchantment, and failure, till we hear the last solemn call to go forth from these things and hear it undismayed.

"All in the wild March morning I heard the angels call;
It was when the moon was setting, and the dark was over all;
The trees began to whisper, and the wind began to roll,
And in the wild March morning I heard them call my soul."

THE WISDOM OF GOD IN A MYSTERY *

DR. WHYTE has written an admirable appreciation of Jacob Böhme. It is perhaps the best thing he has yet published, and only those who know something of Böhme will do justice to the care and thoroughness with which the work has been done. What is far more important in such a connection is sympathy, and of this Dr. Whyte has a full measure. He has a real affinity with the mystics. It is true that Jacob Böhme, by the amazing splendour of his genius, has forced his personality upon all serious thinkers. But the inner circle who regard him with peculiar reverence, the quiet congregation to whom he steadily makes his appeal, read him with other eyes, and they will recognise Dr.

* "Jacob Behmen. An Appreciation." By Alexander Whyte, D.D. (Oliphant, Anderson & Ferrier.)

Whyte as one of themselves. In short, the Edinburgh preacher knows what Böhme is saying. That is enough. Nothing less would have been enough. The mystics understand one another. "Deep calleth unto deep," and the message is understood, though to the outer world it be no more than the chattering of sparrows or the hooting of owls.

The appearance of this little volume gives occasion for some thoughts on the position of mysticism in the Church of Christ. The mystics have never failed us, and sometimes, though very rarely, their influence has been wide and obvious. The critical movement of the present day is not likely to find its legitimate end in mysticism, but mysticism will make its own contribution to the theology of the not far distant future. In the first place, mysticism teaches the entire dependence of the spirit of man on the Spirit of God. The text to which Jacob Böhme especially clave was, "How much more shall your heavenly Father give the Holy Spirit to them that ask Him." Good thoughts, in the mystical view, are the free children of God, and do not come by thinking. "It is not I, but the Spirit of the Lord doth it in such measure as He pleaseth," is the burden of Böhme's profession. In the works of William Law we find the same truth insisted on with even greater emphasis. Reason to Law is the first and last grand deceiver of mankind. A mystery is the deep and true ground of all things. Perhaps, however, it would be correct to say that what impressed Böhme and Law so deeply was not so much the failure of the reason as the failure of nature. They could not have denied the legitimate function of the natural reason among natural things. What struck their hearts with wonder was the absolute failure of the natural man at his highest to come within sight or sound of spiritual things. It may be doubted whether the mystics go further than Our Lord and His apostles. "A man can receive nothing, except it be given him from heaven." St. Paul dwells with profound solemnity upon the mystery of divine knowledge. He spoke the wisdom of God in a mystery, or, as we might say, in a whisper. The substance of his message was mystery, and therefore in form it was also a mystery. True, the great facts of Christian redemption are set before the opening eyes of faith, and whosoever looks is saved. But these facts have around them, above them, beneath them, a rich and subtle philosophy. All the counsel of God, from the eternal election till the final setting of the Church in glory, makes up this wisdom. To understand even the least part of it we need the illumination of the Spirit, and so each scholar in the great school where all Zion's children are taught of God is, like Jesus Christ, a "listener unto death." To the natural man all is darkness; and for the spiritual man even the unveiling is slow. We are, as it were, set in face of a curtain, which is gradually lifted as we gaze in prayer. Whenever we turn away it drops again. To those who have looked long and eagerly it discloses at last the very depths of the sanctities of heaven.

Since this is the way to divine knowledge, we cannot rightly speak of such things as the simple Gospel. There is no simple Gospel. Neither can we draw the frontiers of truth with geometrical exactness. Overmuch definiteness in a creed is a sign of its falsity. As Edward Irving said in his great days, "To my certain knowledge the atmosphere of theology hath been so long clear and cloudless that there hath been neither mist nor rain these many years, and even to talk of a mystery is out of date. But *thou* must preach

Christ in a mystery." Böhmenism had its first vogue in England when a cold and hard Calvinism was dominant. We do not know that sufficient stress has been laid on the fact that some of the English translations of Böhme were published by Giles Calvert, the official publisher to George Fox. The grand passage of George Fox, written at the age of twenty-four, and beginning, "Now was I come up in spirit through the flaming sword," is surely an echo of Böhme, and if this be so, the mystic must be credited with no small share in the origination of Quakerism.

Next, the mystics teach that delight in God is the true happiness of life. In manifold forms they proclaim that all the happiness or misery of all creatures consists only in this, that they are more or less possessed of God, or, as one of the best of them puts it, "We have no want of religion but so far as we want to better our state in God." The object of mysticism is indeed a closer union with the divine. To sink in the depths of God is the crowning, ineffable joy. They claim to have realised it. "The triumph that was then in my soul I can neither tell or describe. I can only liken it to a resurrection from the dead." Böhme says that he found himself in a seven days' soul-sabbath, where he looked into the mystery of God as into an open secret, where he regained the flower of paradise in the new man. Thus possessing God, he possessed nature. As Wordsworth said long after:

> "By grace divine,
> Not otherwise, O Nature, we are thine."

Can it be said that this conflicts with the Bible view of religion? Can it be said that such experiences are common in the Church of to-day? May we achieve such a sense and possession of God as shall carry us over our griefs and help us to do our drudgery with an incredible lightness of heart? Let us not too quickly deny the reality of what the saints have known. "You are disappointed," said the Franciscan to Madame Guyon, "because you seek without what you have within. Accustom yourself to seek God in your heart, and you will find Him." When she ceased from her own works in obedience to this word, God took possession of her soul. She prayed without ceasing. Her heart was filled with a sense of peace and possession. Time was annihilated, and love became the habit of the heart. The books of the mystics are witnesses, whenever faith sinks, of the possibilities open to the believing and surrendered soul.

It almost necessarily follows that the mystics are not always intelligible. The action of mysticism on the spirit may perhaps best be compared to the action of music. It is not possible to put into words all the emotions the high strain raises. Nor is it possible to justify to the man who has no ear the feelings which music excites. In one of his dialogues William Law puts this very well. He says that his neighbour, John the Shepherd, "when he comes home from the field in winter evenings, listens sometimes to the Scriptures and sometimes to Jacob Böhme read by his wife." He confesses that he understands only a little of either, but maintains that, whether he understands or not, the heavenly flame is kindled in his soul. He quotes the lofty words in Revelation which describe the eternal throne, and says, with much justice, that it is better that the heart should be kindled by them to bow down with the elders than that it should trouble about what Hebrew and Greek scholars can tell of the passage. No doubt this may be pushed to extremity. To exclude entirely distinct form and expression from the apprehension of spiritual truth, is to reduce that truth to something like a fire-mist. We start with the Apostles from a disc of really apprehended dogma. The rays reflected are at first not clear. It is only as the spiritual life proceeds that we keep transferring new truths from the region of mysticism to that of clear apprehension, adding all the while to those perceived only in the first stage. Emotion both interprets and transcends language. It takes a catastrophe to bring the tremendous meaning even of the commonest words thoroughly home. How much truer is this of words that try to compass and reveal the experiences of the spirit. The Bible is not anywhere to us what it was twenty years ago. Passages we then passed over as meaningless now take hold of us as with living hands. One may doubt whether the highest spiritual truth will ever go into words. The most poetical region of all, says a living mystic, is that which is incapable of taking the form of poetry. The realities take away the breath that would, if it could, give them forth in song. Some things are impossible to utter, and other things it is unlawful to utter. Over such truths the spirit wanders brooding till it becomes vocal, and that is the utterance we have from mystics. Mysticism is the science of love—that love which supersedes the sacraments, that love which the Apostle saw lasting while tongues ceased, prophecy failed, knowledge vanished away, and the princes of this world came to nought.

Mysticism has often been charged with the establishment of a church within the Church, or rather an *ecclesiola in ecclesia*. This has little relevance so far as Böhme is concerned, for he himself adhered to the Lutheran Church and died in its communion. He did not encourage the establishment of sects. Böhme spoke to the initiated. The phrase, " Enough to those that are Ours " (*Mysterium Magnum*, Gen. xliii. 32), is characteristic.

" God has a few of us whom He whispers in the ear;
 The rest may reason and welcome; 'tis we musicians know."

The idea of a one and only perfect visible Church did not appeal to the mystics. But their *ecclesiola* was rather a *verein* than a *gemeinde*, a religious club rather than a regular church and congregation. The New Testament knows nothing of class religion, and seriously discourages the needless formation of sects. But may it not be suggested that one great need of the present time is that those bent on the re-animation of lingering causes and the revival of forgotten truths should quietly associate themselves together to further the common end? There is too much isolation among us. One man with strong convictions may be able to do something, but if properly reinforced by others of the same mind he might do far more. Dr. Whyte, we have no doubt, agrees with us that mysticism is not meant for the Church at large. He would, however, do great service if he organised the few to whom the subject appeals. If we had space to dwell on this fascinating theme, we should like to say something of the English Böhmenists. Their lives have not been written, nor is there, so far as we know, any clear indication of the two periods when Böhmenism was a power in the religious development of our country.

Whatever be said of his theology and philosophy, no one can deny that Jacob Böhme's portion in life was the enjoyment of God. The story of his beautiful and sacred death cannot be told too often. Shortly after midnight one Sabbath he overheard the worship of the world of spirits. He called his son Tobias, and asked him if he did not hear that sweet, harmonious music. The door was set wide that he might listen more peacefully. Then, smitten with desire, he exclaimed, "O Thou strong God of Sabaoth, deliver me according to Thy will," and immediately afterwards, "Thou crucified Lord Jesus Christ, have mercy upon me, and take me to Thyself in Thy kingdom." A little later the prayer was answered, and with the words, "Now I go hence to Paradise," he entered in. Over his grave at Görlitz, which is still a place of pilgrimage, is inscribed, "Here rests Jacob Böhme, born of God, died in Christ sealed with the Holy Spirit."

THE PRAYER-MEETING

GEORGE MACDONALD describes in one of his books a prayer-meeting or week-day service in a Kentish Town chapel. The preacher was a stickit minister from Scotland. Few people even in the North are now aware of the tragedy that accompanied pulpit failure. In these days of diminished sensitiveness and increased fluency the agony seems inconceivable; but to this stickit minister the hour of anguish, though it had gone past some thirty years, was still vivid. It overshadowed his spirit. He called back the place and the day—a Scotch village, his own village, a golden wind blowing on a wavy harvest morning, little clouds floating in the sunny blue, the church filled with well-known faces upturned and critical. Then came swiftly the moment of collapse when he failed utterly, pitifully, while his mother wept low, and his father clutched hands of despair behind the tails of his Sunday coat. The three went home together in speechless sorrow and despair, and the hour vanished in a slow mist of abject misery and shame. It was only very long after, when he was growing old, that he again opened his mouth to preach Christ, and then it was in circumstances the dreariness of which depressed him. That huge slug *the Commonplace*, the wearifullest dragon to fight in the whole creation, the monster whom you may wound but cannot kill, holds great sway in the north-west of London and was then specially powerful in dissenting chapels. Never more so in his beauty-blasting, depressing power than on the night of the weekly prayer-meeting, and that night a drizzling one. The steaming glare of the yellow lights that filled the lower part of the chapel, the ugly twilight that possessed the yawning galleries, seemed to illuminate the monster whose faintly gelatinous bulk filled the whole place. There were but nine hearers, and at first it seemed as if their faces were but ganglions of the beast. None of them was fit to deal him one of those blows which he suffers from every sunrise, every repentance, every childbirth, and every true love. Stay! there was one, a brooding, careworn countenance of a woman who had a life of labour and vanished children lying behind her. She was racked with the enigma of how to pay her rent, consumed with pitiful worries, and her look gave the preacher strength to tell the story of sun and breeze, of resurrection and uplifting, of organ blasts and exultation which has been written for every spirit which Satan hath bound. At that time there was little suspicion of neology. The monster was growling in German jungles, but could not cross the sea. The preaching gave the poor widow "strength in my heart to bear up, and that is better than money." She was not one to take the kingdom of heaven by force, but one to creep quietly into it if a gentle hand took hers.

From the same region of London, a region which has had a strange fascination for our dissenting writers—for is it not there that Mark Rutherford fixes the story of "The Modern Martyr" who resisted the will to die and went on quietly in spite of the evolutionist correcting exercises in Euclid?—comes another and much more cordial testimony to the helpfulness of the week-night service. Thomas Lynch, whose indomitable spirit never yielded to the misery of his surroundings, his scanty audiences, and his dreary chapels, left behind him a paper on the subject. He urged that men often die of the businesses by which they strive to live. Anxiety dulls, frets, and then kills them. But if a man can walk and talk with his God in the cool of a hot day, the morrow's burden will be less heavy; or if he has a childlike gladness in seeing the evening lamp lighted in the holy place, and in both seeing and smelling the evening incense as it curls heavenward, the air of next morning will be sweeter to him, and its light will awaken him to hope. If in winter time he will sit by the fireside of the church in brotherly love to all saints, he will be less likely to drowse and sigh by his own. And if in summer time he will walk with companions in the garden of the Lord as heaven and earth are communing sweetly and sacredly together in the twilight, he will not walk moodily about his own garden complaining that after all its chief productions are the worm and the caterpillar. This is a good word, and we have no doubt as to the blessing ministered to many souls by quiet little week-evening meetings. We are thinking, however, of services where the main business is not preaching, but prayer. Is it possible that the work of any church can be satisfactorily carried on where prayer is not deliberately organised and practised? Prayer-meetings in the true sense are not week-evening services, in that preaching, save as it helps petitions, is of no account. For a week-evening service it is natural that a minister should seek a large audience. He is to be excused if he presses the duty of attendance upon his people. Where many come there is indubitable proof that his words are prized. Week-evening services, we suppose, cannot be kept up with spirit unless a certain number are present, and we believe that in many places they are abandoned for a large part of the year, and in some given over altogether. This does not apply to the ideal prayer-meeting. It is constituted under the charter of Christ. "If two of you shall agree on earth as touching anything that they shall ask, it shall be done for them of my Father which is in heaven." Two, therefore, form a sufficient and a prevailing meeting for prayer. Neither of them needs to be eloquent, but both must be very much in earnest. To urge people to come to a prayer-meeting seems incongruous. They should be urged to pray, and they should be taught that prayer in the highest sense cannot be single. Then they must be left. If sympathetic souls find their way to the gathering, and are able to enter with fulness of heart into the supplication, great spiritual issues will be decided. On the other hand, to have a number of hearers none of them fully imbued with the spirit and faith of prayer, is an unmitigated calamity. It may be said with confidence that a large prayer-meeting is very often no prayer-meeting.

But surely from every church, even the humblest and poorest, two might be found to make a prayer-meeting. What is the power of two as contrasted with the power of one?

In the first place, when two agree as touching what they shall ask, there is reason to hope that a corrective element will be applied to the petitions. Isolated, we grow selfish; the burden of our own sad need presses upon us too heavily, the lower forms of desire and passion assert their sway. There are, it has been said, three forms of prayer—the evil, the non-moral, and the spiritual. That there are evil prayers—sordid, selfish and base—we know. We doubt whether there are non-moral prayers. For as we are always drawn out in tenderness for any one who we see is looking to us in great expectation and tenderly confiding in us, this must also be true of God. He will grieve a little because we so persistently ask Him for the lower, because we think so much more of meat and drink and clothes for the body than of God and love and truth for the soul. He longs that only we would put things in the right order, and seek the best first; but He knows that we must be guided gently, and so in the New Testament no stern distinction is drawn between temporal and spiritual blessings, and the largest possible encouragement is given to all souls to pray. So much is the encouragement that perhaps nine-tenths of the sermons on prayer consist of warnings not to expect too much. God knows that if we once come close to Him, if our hearts touch His, we shall grow in grace and wisdom, and find that even in the promise the half was not told us. We learn from this contact that prayer prevails not merely in that it subsides into God's will and takes the fact as decided in our faith, but that it brings a reason for God's hearing us and giving the thing requested, as otherwise He would not have a call to do. Besides, what strength and depth of Christian communion there is between two souls that have entered into a true league of prayer, when each is not afraid to unbare to the other his whole heart, and when everything that is merely selfish fades away and is ashamed in the light of the divine love!

Not only is it well that two should agree in prayer because in this way the lower elements of petitions subside, but in ways we cannot fully understand the addition of will to will increases the force of prayer. On this subject Bushnell has some wise remarks. He is commenting on the palmary promises given by Our Lord to importunity. He protests against the exaggeration which demands that we are to renounce all will to begin with, as if the will were part of our human nature which God does not care to see, makes no account of, and will not cherish. True, the will must not push itself on God's will when God's will is known, but we often do not know, and we must hold on with inflexible tenacity until we do. Many of our prayers have no will; they are dawdling, feeble and futile. But Christ commends with especial heartiness the prayer that will take no denial, that does not faint, and that succeeds by importunity. This tenacity is will, and God looks on our will as a central part of our personality. He means to ennoble it, and not to crush it. There are many prayers that can only be answered by the action of a great will force in man. How, for instance, is one to recover health when he discourages soul and body in consenting to have no will about the matter save in prayer? Then it has to be remembered that God is always answering prayer on the ground of the largest reasons. All God's purposes are set by God's reason, even as clocks are by the sun, though the purposes may be as in everlasting counsel before the prayers are made. And so it is not too much to say that God is always considering as to what the most and weightiest things and people agree—where any prayer for health makes as strong a suit as the sensuality and pride petitioning for disease, where so many Christian people praying for the times can pray down what the times themselves invoke. The only true, earnest way of praying is to get as many things to pray with you as possible, and as few to pray against. We may have little power, but surely each of us may find one soul, and when two agree in prayer there is an illimitable promise. We shall try to consider what modification the frank adoption of this great principle would make on the life of our churches.

"IF TWO OF YOU SHALL AGREE"

IN the opinion of some who still profess to be Christians, the idea of asking and receiving from God is a fond superstition or a pitiable weakness. But asking and receiving are of the essence of prayer, and it is no true prayer-meeting where the main attraction is the preaching of short, bright sermons, or even common meditation on divine themes. Neither is it a prayer-meeting where prayer is viewed as a spiritual gymnastic, beneficial to the suppliant, but otherwise of no account. If God is absent, or bound in the chains of inexorable law, there can be no true prayer. And it is the caricature and counterfeit of all devotion to say with some mystics that the will must be annihilated, and that there is no permissible prayer but the Prayer of Silence—*Thy will be done.* Madame Guyon told Bossuet that she was unable to pray for any particular thing—the forgiveness of sins, for instance. To do so was to fail in absolute abandonment and disinterestedness. It is true that we evermore enter into God through death, but God works in man, and not instead of man. Over against this negation we set the teaching of Our Lord and His Apostles, and earnestly seek to break once more the seals of prayer.

"If two of you shall agree." Two are enough to form a prayer-meeting, and what church is so poor as not to be able to furnish them? No machinery is needed, no announcement, nothing but the complete and sacred agreement of two believers. When these come together, they will come to pray. They will doubtless taste the good word of God and the powers of the world to come, that their hearts may be stirred up. They will enter into a profound spiritual friendship, into the inmost depths of one another's souls. They will have much to ask for themselves. But their main business will be intercession, and intercession is at once the highest and most difficult form of prayer. Our Lord Jesus, that Great Shepherd of the sheep, intercedes before the Father, and His sacred function, as Dr. Denney has pointed out, is mentioned by the Apostles with a kind of adoring awe, which is quite peculiar even in the New Testament. "It seems to have impressed them as one of the unimaginable wonders of Redemption, something which in love went far beyond all that we could ask or think. When inspired thought touches it it rests as on an unsurpassable height." The intercession of Christ is the culmination of His priesthood, the crowning act of that love of which the foundations were laid on Calvary. Our intercession is a spark from the altar which burns day and night before the Lord in heaven. And therefore it is not easy, not light, but hard and costly. It is a voice calling from that estate of misery which has no explanation but the Fall and no remedy but the Cross. Real intercession wades as deep as love. It has hours that in their measure are like the Lord's Gethsemane: "I have great heaviness and continual sorrow of heart for my brethren, my kinsmen according to the flesh." The great intercessors of the world are secretly and immediately called by Christ Himself, even as He, the Man of the Cross, was called of God: "I sought for a man among them that should make up the hedge and stand in the gap before me." To suppose that the duty of intercession is fulfilled by attending what is called a hearty prayer-meeting, to suppose that it is completed when a list of names is called over, is fundamentally to misunderstand. Intercession charges itself with the want, the woe, the load, the care, the sin, the anguish of all for whom it pleads.

When two come together for intercession they will, first of all, pray for the church they are representing. Few things are more wonderful than the service of unknown intercessors to humble churches of Christ. How many men and women there have been, whose names were never tossed about in the great world, who had no eloquence and no wealth and no learning, but who by their continual and prevailing prayers made safe and sweet and blessed some corner of God's vineyard on earth! They prayed from the depths of serene and strong hearts, and their prayers were answered. With what profound and passionate affection the very least of our churches is regarded by one or two! How many of them have refused to perish, when it often seemed as if they might go out, like the "cresset's flame that the rough wind slew last night." They have lived because their very dust was dear to some among the saints, and for that they are living still. There are, perhaps, hopeful signs of a great and needed change in our conception of the services of the Church. If we go to church to hear sermons, then the sermons must be worth hearing, and where they are not we are absolved. If we go to be touched by the externalities of worship, the true spiritual stimulus must at last fail us. We must go because there is a special manifestation of God in the personality of Jesus Christ vouchsafed in the Church, because there we are united with one another and with the Lord. Our fellow disciples have received from Christ the glory which the Father gave the Son, and we must enter into fellowship with Christian men if we are to enter deeply into fellowship with God. Every worshipper must think of his fellow-worshippers, must merge his own life in the life of the Church, and thus realise the idea of the communion of saints. To do this it is necessary to attend faithfully the services as far as possible, whether or not the preaching is eloquent and interesting. It should be the continual prayer of the intercessors for the Church that the Church may be a household of faith in which no heart can sorrow or rejoice alone. The New Testament justifies far more emphatic teaching on the necessity of the Church and its institutions than one often listens to. It may be doubted whether prayer or communion with Christ or joy in God or any other great experience of the Christian life can be realised in any full sense by isolated believers. The intercessors of the Church, knowing the Church and its needs, will pray that the life of the Church may be more and more a common life, that the fellowship between the members and Christ may be continually deepened and intensified, and if that prayer is fulfilled there will be no need to ask for more.

Once again. The intercessors must pray for the individuals they know. We cannot love all men in the strict and true sense. As Newman said we may feel well disposed to all men. We may act toward all men in a spirit of love. We may view them as those for whom Christ died. But the real love of man depends on practice, and we must begin by loving those near to us, labouring for them, praying for them, bearing with them, suffering for them. It is in this way that there grows in the heart that root of charity which if small at first may, like the mustard seed, at last overshadow the whole earth. We love God whom we have not seen by loving our brethren whom we see. Week by week we should recall their case. There is one who after a consistent life of many years has fallen into a deep abyss of shame. He has dragged with him others who are innocent, and he is at the point of despair. There is one who is reeling under the shock of sudden and terrible bereavement. There is one who has undergone a business disaster which will alter for him the whole aspects of living. And there are those on whom the great blessedness of life has dawned, or is beginning to dawn. There are those who have ranged themselves on the side of Christ, and there are those whose hearts are growing cold. Who can tell what forces and succours may go forth to all these as the result of intercession?

The Christian Church ought to have in its possession far fuller records of the answer to prayer. But we are not left without witness. In the records of Mrs. Beecher Stowe's life we are told that in her later years her consecration took high forms and she especially devoted herself to intercession. There came a time in her history when one who was very dear to her seemed about to sink away from the faith in which she trusted, and she set herself resolutely to avert this calamity. She put the full force of her intellect to work upon this conflict. Letter after letter found its way from her pen to the foreign town in which scepticism was doing its worst for the soul she loved. She wrote, she reasoned, she argued, she pleaded, in vain. Then she turned to her great faith. She secluded herself from all but God, and set her whole faith to labour for her soul's desire. A few weeks after a letter reached her, saying, "At Christmas-time light came to me. I see things differently now." In the life of Dr. Emmons we read that under a great bereavement which had been seen to impend for some time he was wonderfully calm and peaceful. The secret of his composure was discovered in the fact that some Christians had made a league of intercession and had prayed that his faith might not fail.

There must be many readers of these lines who watch with deep solicitude the little churches with which they are connected. They see that spiritual life in them is languid and low. Perhaps they are undergoing sharp trials and impoverishment. It almost seems as if the strain was too great to be borne any longer. Who will form a league of intercession? It is not enough to pray in secret. Let there be another to make the two —one other at least—and let these two make importunate request to the Father and see whether the tide will not turn and a glorious blessing be granted. It will not, it cannot be without cost to the intercessors, but in the spiritual order according to our sorrow so will be our joy, and so we may understand Our Lord's deep word, "Hitherto ye have asked nothing in my name. Ask and ye shall receive, that your joy may be full." In proportion as the sorrow has been deep, even as it has been the sorrow of the Cross, where the heart of God is written out in blood, so will be the grace and the depth of the joy. Intercession can never lie lightly upon the soul of prayer.

"Two strangers happened to be passing through a town where a great fire was raging.

"One of them sat down at the inn, saying, 'It is not my business,' but the other ran into the flames and saved much goods and some people.

"When he came back his companion asked him, 'Who bade thee risk thy life in this business?'

"He said, 'The brave man who bade me bury seed that it may one day bring forth increase.'

"'But if thou thyself hadst been buried in the ruins?'

"'Then should I myself have been the seed.'"

THE CASTING AWAY OF THEOLOGY*

MISS PHELPS—we call her by her maiden name—is a writer whose work has often the fascination of genius. The peculiar characteristics of New England are strong within her. Those who have read the lives of her father and mother will understand how highly strung her temperament is, with what a proud, lonely, wistful, refusing aspect she has looked upon life. In this new book she has told more of her inner feelings than in any other, for it would be idle to ignore that she has described her father and the scenes of her childhood and youth. Professor Austin Phelps was a religious writer of considerable mark, of great sensitiveness, and of a painful conscientiousness. His life was both marred and purified by continual suffering, and though

* "A Singular Life." By Elizabeth Stuart Phelps. (London: James Clarke & Co.)

his ears were open to many of the highest voices of the world, he held tenaciously by the old theology, and was exercised to the depth of his nature when his college at Andover moved in new directions. His daughter, while cherishing an affectionate veneration for her father's character, partly disagreed with his theology, and partly viewed the problems that vexed him as unimportant. Since his death, she and her husband have busied themselves in various literary experiments, none of them quite successful. Nor is "A Singular Life" to be described as in any way a great book, although it has considerable power. Its fault is its extreme conventionality. The characters are fixed types, described without the least subtlety or discrimination, and the action all proceeds as it might in the world of the imagination. Neither are there touches of power such as we occasionally meet with in "A Struggle for Immortality," and in some of Miss Phelps's poems. Nevertheless, the book is good, pure, wholesome, and spirit-stirring, although we should not have given it prominent notice had it not been for its moral. That moral falls in with the tendency of much current thinking, and it is quite worth while to examine it. The book may be described briefly as a plea for the retention of Christianity and the casting away of theology.

Professor Carruth, of Cesarea College, is described as a man of archangelic nature, full of theology, rigidly orthodox, but so profoundly Christian that sometimes he could not quite act up to his barbarous creed. His wife was a commonplace, motherly old lady; his daughter, Helen Carruth, was a young lady of twenty-five, a bright, deep orange blonde, whatever that may mean, very beautiful, dressed in silk and purple and white lace, fond of her father and mother, but leading her life very much apart from them. In particular she was utterly sick of what she considered the whole miserable business of theology. Up to the somewhat mature age mentioned she had taken no interest in the college and none in the students, and she regarded with mingled impatience and contempt controversies about inspiration, the punishment of the lost, and the like. A remarkable student at this period leaves the college and enters Helen Carruth's life. His appropriate name is Bayard. He is marvellously beautiful, chivalrously brave, theologically unsound, and a man of perfect spiritual honour. It is easy to see that Miss Phelps has modelled him on her idea of Robertson of Brighton. This Mr. Bayard, after beginning a friendship with Miss Carruth, has a call to a small seaport town, but when examined by the council it turns out that he is not sufficiently sound. He thereupon starts a church for himself, which is called the Church of the Love of Christ. He does his duty in various respects, displays much prowess as a pugilist, rescues a man from drowning, lives in shabby lodgings, with, of course, some very fine engravings on the walls, is indifferent about food, devotes his energies to work among the lost, and preaches marvellous sermons. He has great troubles and a miserable salary, but his courage does not fail. In due time Helen Carruth appears on the scene. She and her father and mother spend their summer holiday in Mr. Bayard's town. The professor is working at an article on the state of the unforgiven after death — a subject which appears to Mr. Bayard and Miss Carruth infinitely trivial. Miss Carruth says: "If my father weren't such an angel in private life it wouldn't be so funny. I cannot see what he wants the unconverted to be burnt up for." Mr. Bayard quite agrees, and thinks that he has enough to do with the state of the unforgiven before death. We may mildly venture to suggest that the Saviour Jesus Christ whom Bayard is supposed specially to honour, and His Apostle St. Paul, and many others whose lives were a straight and thoughtful journey in their track, were very deeply exercised about the state of the unforgiven after death. But this may pass. In due time Miss Carruth becomes a worker in Mr. Bayard's church, while he throws himself into a fierce battle against the liquor trade, which was cursing the town. He confesses his love for her, but does not propose to marry, as his salary is so small. She goes with her father and mother to Berlin. That amiable lunatic of a professor is actually engaged in studying the question of the authenticity of the fourth Gospel and the effect of German rationalism on the evangelical faith. These trivialities give him peaceful and plentiful occupation, and when after a stormy passage the family returns, Bayard is able to propose marriage, his uncle having left him a house in Boston. They are married accordingly, and very shortly after Bayard is killed by a stone which an angry publican flung at him. The moral of the book is that colleges should give up teaching theology, that ministers should give up studying and preaching it, that the simple Gospel of the love of Christ ought to be declared in a free and unencumbered manner, and that ministers should be prepared for their work by the study of Socialism and the condition of the poor. Let us look at these contentions.

Bayard called his church the Church of the Love of Christ. He stood up in his pulpit week after week and declared that God was love, that Christ loved each soul in his congregation, and would fain strain it to His bosom. What does this involve? In the first place who is Christ? He is unseen—that we know. He has been dead nearly two thousand years—that we know. He is no more among us in the flesh as He was in Palestine. Then who is He whose love has power to pass through the veil and the gate and the silence of death, and touch and warm us now? Who would preach the Gospel of the love of Abraham or of Moses or of Paul? What is there about Christ that puts Him in an altogether different category from theirs, and gives Him power to help us to-day? The answer is, we suppose, that Christ is God. Is not this theology? What happened after Christ's death that gave Him power to reach us with His love as the others who have died cannot? He rose again. Is not this also theology? We seem already to be dealing with two articles of the Christian creed, the Incarnation and the Resurrection, for without these the proclamation that Christ loves the human souls that live is a mockery. And how do we know that Christ loves us? The answer, we suppose, is that His heart was revealed in the Cross, and does not that give us the doctrine of the Atonement? In other words, the inscription, the Church of the Love of Christ, is a ghastly deception unless it rests upon the fundamental articles of the Christian creed—unless, in other words, it has a theology behind it. Nor is that the whole. It may be answered, We know that Christ loved us by the gracious words that proceeded out of His mouth; was it not He who said, "Let not your heart be troubled, neither let it be afraid"? But then did He say these words, or were they the invention of some other? Is not this that very question of the authenticity of the fourth Gospel of which Miss Phelps speaks with such magnificent scorn?

More than this. We need to go far into theology before we can make the belief of the love of God vivid or tenable to mankind. Some, perhaps many, have no difficulty in believing it. To them existence is a sweet, prolonged summer. But the more the facts of life are dragged into the daylight and studied, the deeper is the conviction in thoughtful minds that from these, taken as they stand, the love of God and the righteousness of God cannot be surely discovered. When we come to know God in Christ, we look upon all things in the light of reconciling love, and we apprehend in "the joined and four-squared truth" the wonderful and majestic laws of storm which work surely to a just and clear issue, though they work so slowly. We are able to interpret what we do not know by that which we are sure of, and we find ourselves re-echoing the mild wisdom of Dorothy Winthorp in "Silas Marner."

"But what come to me as clear as the daylight, it was when I was troubling over poor Bessy Fawkes, and it allays comes into my head when I'm sorry for folks, and feel as I can't do a power to help 'em, not if I was to get up i' the middle o' the night—it comes into my head as Them above has got a deal tenderer heart nor what I've got—for I can't be anyways better nor

Them as made me; and if anything looks hard to me, it's because there's things I don't know on; and for the matter o' that, there may be plenty o' things I don't know on, for it's little as I know— that it is. And so, while I was thinking o' that, you come into my mind, Master Marner, and it all come pouring in— If *I* felt i' my inside what was the right and just thing by you, and them as prayed and drawed the lots, all but that wicked 'un, if *they*'d ha' done the right thing by you if they could, isn't there Them as was at the making on us, and knows better and has a better will? And that's all as ever I can be sure on, and everything else is a big puzzle to me when I think on it. For there was the fever come and took off them as were full-growed, and left the helpless children; and there's the breaking o' limbs; and them as 'ud do right and be sober have to suffer by them as are contrairy—eh, there's trouble i' this world, and there's things as we can niver make out the rights on. And all as we've got to do is to trusten, Master Marner—to do the right thing as fur as we know, and to trusten. For if us as knows so little can see a bit o' good and rights, we may be sure as there's a good and a rights bigger nor what we can know

—I feel it i' my own inside as it must be so. And if you could but ha' gone on trustening, Master Marner, you wouldn't ha' run away from your fellow-creatures and been so lone."

But Silas Marner could not take home the reasoning until there was given to him the love of a little child. How many there are who have no solace save the thought that there must come an end at last of their numbered miles of pain! For them the winter will never be past, the rain will never be over and gone, the time of the singing of birds will never come. Never beneath those skies. And even to the most faithful in sight of the terrific tragedies of life, does it not often seem as if the will of the devil were being done on earth even as it is in hell, as if the kingdom of God could never come? Yes, the Christian preacher must be very sure of his ground when he stands up before a company of men and women weighted with sorrow, crushed with care, tortured by remorse, and tells them that each individual has a place in the sacred heart of Christ.

In fact there is one firm foundation, and only one. God commendeth His love toward us in that while we were yet sinners Christ died for us. That is the Gospel of the Cross with which St. Paul confronted Jew and Greek, and it will be found in time either that the preacher must meet his hearers with that message, or cease to speak. It is idle, very idle, to discuss whether in the nature of the case the Apostles could be as perfect organs of revelation as Our Lord Himself. The question is not whether St. Paul occasionally rabbinises, not whether certain among his lines of reasoning are untenable. The question is whether the doctrines with which the Epistles are threaded through and through as a leaf is threaded by its fibres are true or false. If they are true, then there is yet a heart to the world. The Church of God is ransomed and the Church of God is safe. If they are not true, then the Apostles corrupted Christianity and all but destroyed it, and we must tear out their writings from the New Testament before we can hope to get a glimmer of the Christianity of Christ again. But are they false? Let us consider what is put in their stead. If God gave Christ and Christ gave Himself as the propitiation for our sins, then we are on adamant which cannot be shaken. But if not, if Christ died as a martyr, then the proclamation of His love has no meaning; then

Calvary, instead of lifting the gloom from the world, deepens it into despair. If Christ died willingly to atone for our sins, all martyrdoms are explained and glorified. If sin overwhelmed Him, then God has been defeated by evil, and His Cross is the tragedy of the world. The Cross, we know, was victory. He overcame the world in His dying, and no matter what appearances may be, the final triumph of the love of God is there to eyes that have seen the Lord and His Sabaoth.

"German rationalism." We grant that the phrase has often been used very idly and very foolishly. We can understand Miss Phelps's impatience with it. But we assure her that there is a rationalism which is altogether fatal to faith, and that she is drifting in its direction. She has a noble and believing nature. Of her it is eminently true that she has recognised "the dark power of the gods of sorrow, and the sacredness of unbending death." She has done more than this; she has acknowledged the power of the name of Jesus, and she has crowned Him Lord of all. It is grievous that such a woman should join in ignorant and foolish gibes at scholars and their studies, when a very little thinking would enable her to see that, unless our faith rests on certain great facts, Christianity is a ruin and a dream; and that if these facts are true, they necessarily take the form of a theology. As for those whose Gospel is that Christ lived once in Palestine, and that there are valuable sentences to be traced to Him, and that with a little care almost all the familiar verses of the New Testament can be used with the original meaning taken out of them, it needs no prophet to foretell the fate of a church controlled by such. It will live just as long as it is not found out. When it is found out, it will be swept from the earth as an organised hypocrisy.

IS THE GOSPEL OF CHRIST FORGOTTEN?

BEHIND the fact, that in many parts of England the masses are alienated from all Churches, there may be another and even a graver truth. Let us ask, without attempting to answer the question, Is the Gospel of Christ preached generally in our sanctuaries? Or has it been for the time lost and forgotten?

The question may be put in another form. If a preacher discourses in the following fashion, is he declaring the Christian Gospel? "Christ has come to reveal the glory of the higher personal life. Our ideals have been too poor, too near, and too partial. Let us take Christ as the measure of the stature of the perfect man. Let us seek to drink in constantly the spirit of His life. Let our life be an everlasting ascent, through all failure and defeat, to the height on which He stands. Let us be impatient of everything that comes short of the highest, and let us spare no effort to attain it, though it be with wearied feet and bleeding brow and heart loaded with sorrow. Let us wait for the gales of the Spirit, and let us seek to be driven before them. If there is a virtue we would emulate or a fault we would discard, let us gaze on the one till our souls have risen under it as the tide under the moon, or scourge the other in sight of all our faculties till every natural sense recoils from its company. Let us never be stopped by falls. Let us arise from all these, and repent and address ourselves anew to the great task, until the yawning gulf between the actual and the ideal is bridged at last. So yearning, so striving, we are climbing the hill of God, and we are in the way of salvation."

Supposing this were preached to a Christian congregation, would there be any repudiation, any revolt, any clear feeling that the Christian Gospel had been denied? Is it too much to say, even when we are fully willing to distinguish between the constant which we ought to keep and the transient which we ought to let slip, that this, if the New Testament is true, is the negation of Christianity? For what is this but the righteousness of the law, by which no flesh can be saved? It is indeed presented in a lofty fashion. The moral consciousness has been strengthened and purified by the long centuries of Christian history. The doctrine of justification by works cannot any longer be proclaimed in its lower form, for the spiritual sense and craving of mankind have been sharpened, and would not accept it. Nevertheless, in the end of the day, it is the old falsehood which the whole strength of the Apostles was spent in refuting. Virtue under this creed is not created from the order of an inner faith and love; it is ultimately obedience to a formula, and not the natural action of a reconstructed soul. Righteousness is obtained by the effort and struggle of the spirit, and not by the atonement of the Lamb of God. If this is generally preached, then the battle of the Reformation has to be fought over again.

We are very far indeed from saying that those who preach in this fashion reject the true faith. Rather we believe it will come with a shock of surprise to many of them that their teaching has run in this mould. Spiritual faith may and does remain under expressions that fit it very ill, for certainly the Church, now and in all ages, is justified by faith. Nor would we deny—nay, we are eager to admit—that the new legalism is in many instances the fruit of an intelligible reaction against the heresy of heresies, antinomianism, or has taken rise in a righteous impatience of low ideals of the spiritual life. To what extent this reaction has gone we have no means of saying. There are, however, a few tests that may be applied. Wherever the higher legalism is at work, it will be noticed that the doctrine of the Apostles sinks into the background. The thought of righteousness by faith loomed so large in the mind of St. Paul as nearly to cover the whole horizon, and it is natural that he should be patronised or let alone or contradicted by those to whom that doctrine is meaningless. It is no wonder that they cry, "Back to Christ," and take refuge in certain words of Our Lord which a criticism largely subjective is allowed to choose. For the preaching of the righteousness of the law, in however lofty or exalted a manner, makes the greater part of the New Testament, not only meaningless, but glaringly and mischievously untrue. Further, where such views have sway the expiatory death of Christ sinks into the background, and practically ceases to be preached.

Where His dying is referred to, it is expounded in its magnificence as a revelation of sorrow and self-sacrifice. And that is all there is to say. A third test, applicable in cases where the mischief has not gone so far, is that all the attendants on Christian worship are treated as if they were in the fold of Christ. Appeals to the unconverted, prayers for the unconverted, practically disappear from the service. The old rousing words, "Repent," "Believe," never ring from the pulpit. And this is perfectly natural and logical. For if righteousness come by the law, the mere attendance in a Christian sanctuary is proof that the divine life has begun. The feet have been set at the bottom of the ascent, and the preacher sees before him men and women and children who are in different stages of progress and need to be helped in their advance. But to the Evangelical preacher some are in the Way and others are out of it. Some have received the Truth and others are betrayed by falsehood. Some are living and some are dead. All other distinctions sink into insignificance beside this. All steps are nothing in comparison with the process of convulsion and re-creation by which those who are without hope and without God in the world become fellow citizens of the saints and heirs of the grace of life. It is impossible that any preacher, duly burdened with a sense of this appalling contrast, should ever long forget it in preaching or in praying. Yet it would seem from the practice of many Christian ministers that in their view the lost are never to be found within the House of God.

That this teaching can never permanently hold the Church of Christ, and can never in any degree hold it without destroying its force, may be easily proved. There is, as we have said, the great and powerful testimony of the New Testament. But will proof texts in these days subdue the minds of men and turn the course of their thought? Will they not say that if the idea has not survived, and survived in its old regnant place in the Christian Church, it is vain to revive the words in which it was first clothed? Is not the relation between ideas and words this, that the words depart and the ideas remain? Is it not so, that the spiritual structure is not built till the scaffolding has been taken away? Now, we say in reply that though this may be and is generally true, it does not apply to the words of the New Testament. They are spirit and they are life.

Or to turn to modern testimonies, they are, in the phrase we are never weary of quoting, the last words that can be said. They are words which, whenever brought in and allowed time enough to act, are found to fill the house with a deathless fragrance. They are words, to change the figure, which whenever our thoughts touch, they are made perfectly whole. There is a vitality in the very words of Scripture which acts for itself, even when he who speaks them has little or nothing to bring of his own. When the Gospel has died out amongst the rich and powerful, amongst the great and wise, it has been found again and again that the humble Christian evangelist has changed the face of things by a proclamation of the old message, of the message received into his heart.

We might appeal also to the history of the Church. The whole record of Christian life and death has been moulded by the great truth of justification by faith. What Martin Luther calls the true and holy and godly desperation of Staupitius has been to countless thousands their crowning experience. "I have vowed above a thousand times that I would become better, but I have never performed that which I vowed.

Hereafter I will make no such vow, for I have now learned from experience that I am not able to perform it. Unless, therefore, God be favourable and merciful unto me for Christ's sake, and grant unto me a blessed and happy hour, when I shall depart out of this miserable life, I shall not be able, with all my vows and all my good deeds, to stand before Him." That "blessed and happy hour" has been given thousands and thousands of times in the death-beds of believers, as in his, one of the greatest lights of modern culture, who said that over the river of death there was no bridge but the bridge of the Saviour.

But we are willing to admit that these testimonies are not sufficient of themselves. If it can be shown that these truths are needed no longer, then it is not enough to say that they have been needed hitherto. It may be, it is at least theoretically conceivable, that W. R. Greg is correct when he says, "We only require steadily to go right at once and henceforth in order ere long to cancel the consequences of having gone wrong for such countless generations." If it can be shown that there is no weakness and no yearning to which these divine revelations now come with any satisfaction, then the hour has arrived when we must discard the Christian Gospel, and in the words of the writer from whom we have just quoted, look forward no longer to the glorious appearing of Jesus, but to "the advent of a man filled and fired with the enthusiasm of humanity, the prophet of a great yet realisable ideal." But if we can show that the constant needs of man place us in relation with the true, divine things, whether we will or no, then our end has been accomplished. Beliefs cannot die if they have their roots in the nature of man. If they have no such roots, die they will and must.

Where are we to look for the involuntary revelation of the heart? Where are we to look for a true expression of the permanent interests of humanity? Sydney Dobell, in his eloquent essay on the Brontës, anticipated that in the sure and silent social revolution which is to give a new and perpetually renewing aristocracy, and with it a reorganisation of so many popular forms of thought, there will be needed and will arise some great novelist as a chief apostle. Poets, whenever they are prophets, can only speak to the highest. In doctrines and practices appealing to every man, wise and foolish, rich and poor, old and young, the highest genius and the lowest drudge, the evangelist, like the evangel, must be cosmopolitan. More than forty years have passed since these words were written, and it cannot be said that the novelist, who is also a prophet, has yet arisen. But more and more in our day the novelist has become cosmopolitan. The literature of fiction is the daily bread of multitudes, and in common justice it must be allowed that some of these writers, who are most opposed to Christianity, have taken their work with true seriousness, have not said "Peace, peace" when there was no peace, have recognised that there are elements in our society of infallible disruption and revolution. They may not speak to us from a height. They may speak rather, in Dobell's phrase, in thick thoroughfares of our Lystras, but they have a message, and a message which the Christian teacher ought to know and seriously consider. They proclaim, if not the remedy, at least the disease. They cry out for the ills that still afflict us in the midst of our boasted progress. They testify to the hunger of the heart and the thirst of the spirit and the nakedness of the whole nature. They mourn because the whole head is sick and the whole heart faint. We shall try to find the meaning of their plaint, and to see whether it is not a cry for Christ in His perfect righteousness and His atoning love.

"CAST YOUR DEADLY DOING DOWN"

WE have asked whether there was not a return to that preaching of a righteousness by the law which the New Testament is written to condemn. We admitted that if this preaching reached its aim, there was no more to be said. Testimony and experience might be pleaded vainly in face of an altered human nature. But is human nature altered? Carlyle, it has been said, made out that man's nature is only spiritual on the side of its wants. Well, that is something; nay, it is very much. Do the old cravings remain and assert themselves, the cravings for which there is no answer save in the Holy Gospel? We shall take our reply from those who are outside of the Church, but who strive after a deep and serious understanding of human nature and human life.

It may conduce to clearness if we give the old teaching in what seems to many its most offensive and uncompromising form. Mr. Froude in one of his essays describes a revival meeting at which he heard a hymn which he thinks it worth while to quote as a sample and proof of the immorality of evangelicalism. These are the words :

> " Nothing either great or small,
>   Nothing, sinner, no :
> Jesus did it, did it all,
>   Long, long ago.
>
> When He from His lofty throne
>   Stooped to do and die,
> Everything was fully done—
>   Hearken to the cry
>
> ' It is finished ! ' Yes, indeed,
>   Finished every jot.
> Sinner, this is all you need,
>   Tell me, is it not ?
>
> Weary, working, toiling ones,
>   Wherefore toil ye so ?
> Cease from doing ; all was done
>   Long, long ago.
>
> Till to Jesus you can cling
>   By a simple faith,
> Doing is a deadly thing,
>   Doing ends in death.
>
> Cast your deadly doing down.
>   Down at Jesus' feet.
> Stand in Him, in Him alone,
>   Gloriously complete."

These lines may be thought an expression, so sincere and poignant as almost to rise into poetry, of the fundamental truth of the Gospel. The phrases in it which apparently most provoke anger and scorn are these: "Doing ends in death," and "Cast your deadly doing down."

These words have been taken, and that by accredited ministers of Christ, as deliberate incentives to immorality.

For answer we shall not go back upon the records of spiritual experience. We shall not quote from these stories of vain attempts after the righteousness of the law which are among the most burning pages in all literature, so terrible in their intensity that one seems rather to hear a penitent sobbing out a confession with white lips and bursting sighs than to read a quiet page at a quiet table. But we turn to ask the prophets of our time what their experience has been. Let us begin on the level of ordinary secular experience. A man desires to be a poet. He studies the rules of grammar. He masters the principles of melody. He acquires a rhyming dictionary and stocks his memory with jingles. He even acquires familiarity with the works of the masters. All that labour can do is done.

All that teaching can give is given. Is he then a poet? Take Ibsen's answer in one of his early works.

"*K. Skule.* Tell me, Jatgier, how came you to be a bard? Who taught you the art?

"*Jatgier.* The art cannot be taught, sire.

"*K. Skule.* It cannot be taught? Then how came it?

"*Jatgier.* One gave me the gift . . ."

Or we may take the case of a painter. A man desires to learn the mystery of art. Teachers can do something for him, and they take him on as far as they can lead him. He masters the *technique* so far as his capacity extends. The whole mechanism is revealed to him, and, so far as rules can make him, he is a painter. But what then? Sir Joshua Reynolds once examined a painting, and at the end of his scrutiny, said significantly, "It wants—THAT." "THAT" meant everything. It wanted life, soul, quality, potency—all.

It would be both useless and tedious to accumulate illustrations. They may be gathered from every sphere, and has it not begun to dawn on the mind of the reader that we are coming back to the rude phrases of the hymn-writer?

Is it not so that we say to the man who seeks to be poet or painter by rule, "Doing is a deadly thing," "Cast your deadly doing down"? This is the counsel of every master in the schools of art. And are we not coming closer still to the words of St. Paul, "If there had been a law given which could make life, verily righteousness would have been of the law"? But because no law has been given that can make life, righteousness, perfection, achievement have never been possible by obedience to rule, and the end of mere obedience to rule is frustration and defeat.

Is it otherwise in the sphere of morals? We take two witnesses, one of whom at least will not be suspected of Christian leanings. Mr. George Bernard Shaw, a very clever and unsparing critic, has pointed out with much penetration that it is possible for a man to pass the moral catechism, Have you obeyed the commandments? have you kept the law? and at the end to live a worse life than the sinner who must answer "nay" through all the questions. But substitute for this catechism another in which the one point to be settled is "guilty or not guilty," and the whole world is condemned before

God. Again, the ablest expositor of Browning declares that the poet by implication rejects the view ordinarily held without being examined, that the moral life is preliminary to the joy and rest of religion. The same writer says, echoing his master, that morality is the sphere of discrepancy, and the moral life is a progressive realisation of a good that can never be complete. It would thus seem to be immeasurably different from religion, which must in some way or other find the good to be present, actual, absolute, without shadow of change, or hint of limit and imperfection. It will serve to clearness if we analyse the answer of the deeper sceptical thought of our time to the pretence that righteousness may come by the law.

In the first place, the greater modern sceptics have joined with the Christian Church in confessing the depravity of human nature. Browning is not to be quoted in this connection, though he was led to Christianity because it " taught original sin, the corruption of man's heart." But he viewed human nature at its worst in the spirit of an apostle. We turn rather to the one writer of great imaginative genius left to us (with the possible exception of Tolstoi)—we mean the

Norwegian dramatist, Ibsen. All kinds of morals have been drawn from Ibsen's plays, and the critics will long be free to pick and choose. But the truer view is that Ibsen does not mean to be a moralist, but only to describe. He insists that his readers should dare to face facts and recognise reality. The business of Ibsen has been to tear off the last mask from the unbearable face of truth. Because he has done so, his writings have been received with howls of execration. He has been charged with only caring to see what is foul, mean, and repulsive. He has suffered from the wrath kindled by the presence of a traitor among the conspirators of silence. Second thoughts have chastened and sobered his severest censors, and they have gone from him with their glib optimism rebuked. Yes, it is true; evil has penetrated the last recesses of man's life. "Who told thee that thou wast naked?" This comes from eating of the tree of the knowledge of good and evil. Monstrous as many of its performances have been, we are inclined to think that the realistic school in the closing years of this century has, as a whole, made for righteousness by making for unwelcome truth. It has been possible at various periods to

L

cover up the whole action of society under conventional disguises. But, as Mark Rutherford says, behind the walls there were secret passages and staircases by which men gained access to freedom. We repeat that the scepticism of serious men in our day is entirely with the Church in maintaining that evil is the dominant power in human life. The good is overmatched, and therefore at the start the effort to obtain righteousness by the law is doomed to failure.

But scepticism does not accept the fact in the spirit of Christianity. Renouncing the overcoming hope of Christ, it has to find such anodynes and palliatives as are possible. Perhaps in the best minds the first result is contentment with low ideals of goodness. It soon grows weary of " the strain that bids nor sit nor stand, but go." No one has ever preached more earnestly than W. R. Greg against the base confusion between Paradise and the pig-sty. Few modern writers have got such glimpses of a possible moral glory, and yet this really spiritual writer comes at last to hope that men may attain the measure of the stature of—William and Robert Chambers! This is a " realisable ideal." The people may become as hardy, enduring, and ambitious as the better specimens of the Scotch peasants, and they may value instruction as much. That is the end of all dreams! To be successful in the ordinary struggle for wealth and responsibility, to be content with an existence which after all is essentially money-making and mundane! Greg himself, it is just to say, fretted restlessly against such a climax as this. But his reasonable hopes carried him very little further. We are very far from disparaging the virtues of the eminent Edinburgh publishers. But when we yield to these hopes, which ought to be called despairs, are we not back again in the days when David Hume led the world out of the shadow of eternity and showed that it was only an object of the five senses, or of six, if we add hunger? Are we not back again in the days when, as a writer says, the divine element was explained away and the proper study of mankind was not man, as that age thought, but man reduced to his beggarly elements, a being animated by the sensuous springs of pleasure and pain, who should properly, as Carlyle thought, go on all fours? The end is that political economy supplants ethics, religion gives way to naturalism, and poetry to prose. Or, as the hero of one of Ibsen's plays concludes:

"The requirements of this life are hopelessly irreconcilable with high faith and lofty principle, and man must choose between being sordidly practical and nobly fanatical."

Again, the tendency of this scepticism is to despair of moral progress. Those who are affected by it never believe in the good results of missions. They scoff at the thought of sudden moral transformation. They have no expectation of permanently raising the fallen. The picture of human nature given by St. Paul in the beginning of Romans is instructively confirmed by that of Juvenal. But, as has been pointed out, the contrast of their inferences is even more remarkable. It was the same corruption of society that wearied out the Satirist and made the Apostle say, "I must see Rome." He was conscious evermore of possessing the spell that could subdue its worst corruption.

The lowest deep is the palliation and ultimate denial of sin. When dreams are dust and hope is dead, it seems needless to correct or to restrain animal instincts. The sceptic is brought at last to a confession of ethical agnosticism, and the only sin comes to be the sin of passing a moral judgment. One of the most powerful stories of our time is entitled "Tess of the D'Urbervilles, a pure woman faithfully presented." The writer has followed it by another book, in which he seems to echo a saying in Ibsen, "Follow after God or deny Him—either way thy deeds are doomed." The empire of the spirit thus falls a prey to the empire of the flesh. A daring writer of that school says that all morality is relative. Whether a woman is to be chaste or not depends as much upon circumstances as whether she shall call a cab or walk. He goes on to declare that duty is the primal curse, from which we must redeem ourselves before we can advance another step on the road. God, once the most sacred of our conceptions, has been denied; reason, the infallible Pope, has been defied; and duty, according to this writer, is not more sacred than God or reason. He is right when he further affirms that the terms of realist morality have not yet appeared in our living language.

Do the words of the hymn seem quite so strange? Is it not true that "doing is a deadly thing," that "doing ends in death," that righteousness cannot come by the law because the law cannot give life, and that those who refuse to seek the life above the law must die? The true standard and unquenchable hope of goodness is in Christ, who died and rose again, and sat down incarnate at the right hand of God.

We have given one side of the argument against the possibility of a legal righteousness. Another remains to be dealt with.

IS CHRIST DEAD IN VAIN?

IS the death of Christ to be counted for as little in His life as death is in ours? He might have died in peace and at a good old age for all that many modern pulpits say. But this was not the fashion of His dying. It was early and cruel and purposed. We have seen week how the New Testament argues against a righteousness by the law on the ground that the law cannot give the strength which is necessary for obedience. Terrible is the mountain of Moses, more terrible is the mountain of Christ, with calls and commandments which human nature vainly strives to fulfil. We pointed out the deep consciousness of failure expressed in modern literature, and the analogy which there is between vain efforts to achieve ethical perfection without a new force acting on the life, and the equally vain efforts to acquire by compliance with rule a skill in art which is only possible to those who possess the initial gift. Another line of argument turns on the significance of the death of Christ. That death is the great fact in the history of the world. But if righteousness come by the law, it is inexplicable, useless. Christ is dead in vain. Is there then a constant need in the heart of man, only met by this offering up of the Lord Jesus? Supposing we could vanquish sin for the future by an immense act of will, can the old tangled skein be disentangled? The answer is that it cannot. No conviction is burned more deeply into the inner heart of the world than this, that sin is not done with us when we have done with sin. There are men and women by the hundred thousand who would gladly give all they possess if they could but lay their hands upon one hour of madness and pluck it from the past.

It is often asserted that the sense of sin in our generation is very weak, and in fact almost extinct. That sin itself has been weakened in proportion nobody affirms. In any case God has not left Himself without a witness. If the sense of sin is not strong, the sense of misery is keener than ever. Surely no age since Christ came has been more sick at heart than ours.

Amidst the splendours of outward prosperity and the abandonment of faith and responsibility, gladness has almost died out. Wherever serious joy and peace survive, it is on Christian soil.

The outstanding facts which forbid the hope of righteousness by the law are those of retribution and remorse. Men may sneer at "the great cat Fate and her random selection of victims," but no belief more obstinately persists than the belief in a moral order, in the inevitable punishment of transgression. The moral nature must be satisfied by a moral rule. It is even true to say that in a great degree the consequence of a moral nature is a moral rule. So long as men believe in goodness they will desire to befriend the righteous and to thwart the wicked, and in that fashion to make themselves the instruments of the divine purpose. Outside of Christianity, and indeed everywhere almost, among all tongues and kindreds, men have declined to rest in the troublous thought that the ungodly are not plagued like other men. A survey of the facts of life has brought them to "absolve the gods." "Who is he," exclaimed the ancients of Thebes—"who is he whom the Delphic rock of prophecy has denounced as the doer of deeds unutterable, the man of the bloody hand? Time it is that he should flee with foot swifter than the horses of the winds. Already hath the son of Jove taken arms against him. Even hot thunderbolts and the fearful fates follow after, and who shall escape them?" "And when the barbarians saw the venomous beast hang on the hands of Paul, they said among themselves, 'No doubt this man is a murderer, whom though he hath escaped the sea, yet *vengeance suffereth not to live.*'" This strong belief has continually fortified itself in the face of much that might seem to stagger it. It has led to countless observations like this, that the pen and ink with which Charles signed the death-warrant of Lord Strafford was the very same with which he signed his own, in the Bill for the Long Parliament. Indeed, the general disposition to construe calamities into judgments, however inaccurate in many cases, witnesses to the enduring and ineradicable strength of the conviction.

Even when retribution is delayed there is the fact of remorse. Though the evil deed may not for a time take bodily form and confront the doer of it as a material fact, there is a spiritual cage of unclean birds in which it is ordained the soul should sit. When the feverish happiness and the stark insensibility have had their time, the accretions of habit and custom fall away, the disguising veils are rent, and that image of the Son, to which we were to be conformed, gazes on us accusingly. The fact of remorse is written broadly, profoundly, over the whole face of modern unbelieving literature. "I had nothing of the nature of conscience till then, and therefore I could feel no remorse, and now this is the truth of the whole matter, I am a perpetual prey to remorse. I cannot get that wretched Evelyn out of my head. A wrong done lasts for ever. I never realised that before as I do now. That horrible cry of hers lingers in my ears, and her white face."

And although remorse may be deferred for a period, deterioration begins the instant after sin. There may be a dreadful complacency and content as friendship becomes mercenary and home squalid, and love animal and everything sinks down out of its nobleness. The perception may seem hopelessly blunted, and the soul may take to all sensual delight, saying not, "Let us eat and drink, for to-morrow we die," but "Let us eat and drink, for to-day we are dead." But sooner or later the revealing hour arrives. We come to know as in a flash the depths of the abyss we have descended. And at last the tongues of fire clasp the heart.

Where is the escape from this? Is it not matter of sober fact that only the religion of Jesus has sought to answer this question, that Christianity alone of all religions has fairly measured itself with retribution and remorse? The tendency, increasing in later years, is to look to the "mild gate of death," not very far away from any, and indeed within a step of all. Those on whom the unbearable misery of the world lies heavily, glorify death as the great peacemaker, the friend to be counted on who never fails any one. And they try to believe that in death is the final and complete payment of the wages of sin. But something protests against this. The obstinate will to live keeps many, who are indeed most wretched, from suicide. For what if death does not end all? What if, with terror-stricken hearts, sinners may meet on the other side the old humanity which death could not kill and take up for ever the old battle and burden-bearing, which it would seem as if no man could escape so long as he is man? An age like ours, which can believe that there are malicious and cruel powers above us, cannot find it so very difficult to believe that these powers may bring us through death and still torment us on its other side. It was said long ago by a very acute critic—and we incline to think it is true—that Bishop Butler in his "Analogy" did not need to assume a belief in the being of God. The real necessary starting-point is in the facts of experience. Whether or not there is one great personal first Cause, such and such is the consequence of things in the world of experience, and therefore it may well be similar to this in the next world. Such and such are the relations to one another of the successive stages of life here, and therefore there may well be similar relations between this life and that to come—such and such is the weakness of the presumption that death is the cessation of existence, therefore the ground is clear for the direct proofs that we shall live hereafter.

But Christianity tells us that Christ has died to take away our sins, and it speaks first to our sense of remorse. It brings to us a sense of pardon. Is it the experience of our readers that they hear much of this in the preaching of to-day? If not, practically the whole content of the Christian Gospel has been omitted. Our sins are forgiven us for His name's sake. We who have believed do enter into rest. The past has been blotted from the memory of God, and the soul is at home in the bosom of atoning love. That is the primal fact. The New Testament does not say much, though it says more than might be supposed, of absolution from earthly penalty. It does not define what God can or will do among the shackling chains of inevitable cause and effect. But even if the consequences are unaltered, they are endured in a new atmosphere of love which allays and soothes their pain, and the suffering is not judicial punishment, neither is it the uncontrollable working out of forces set in motion by sin. It is under the measure and administration of God the Father. Believing, we pass from the world of fixity into the world of life. Other lords, the forces of law, stern, absolute, merciless, have had dominion over us, now the Son has made us free indeed. The adamantine chain has been broken in the liberty of redemption, and we have entered into the freedom of Christ's life and work and death. Protestant theology is as yet far behind Roman Catholic theology in its handling of the great doctrines of Solidarity, Reversibility, and Expiation. But it is much, very much, to enter into the joyful consciousness of reconciliation, and to understand that nothing more can happen to us that does not come in love and blessing, and that the long agony between sin and grace will end at last in the perfect and everlasting triumph of love.

It follows that the doctrine of the Atonement must not be discussed *in vacuo*. It cannot be argued out like a mathematical proposition to the satisfaction of those who do not need it. It is understood where it is needed, and only there. To know it, we must first grapple in earnest with the immense terror of eternal ruin. The spirit, if the expression may be allowed, must be flayed, and thus offer a surface quick to the lightest touch. Then the great message of the Gospel is comprehended in its everlasting fulness and simplicity. It needs no commendation, no explaining. It meets the whole wants of the guilty. The offering of the Lord Jesus will be comprehended by the saints more fully as the years advance. Since the awful day on which He died, it has opened before each generation new abysses of significance. It has manifested more and more wondrously the exceeding riches of God's grace.

And it meets a constant need, a need which has no other answer, to which no other answer is even attempted. If preachers are taking in these times to a sublimated system of Christian ethics, if they have practically discarded the whole Christian revelation except the Sermon on the Mount, the Church may still live, for there is such virtue in Christ that even to touch the hem of His garment is to be healed. But the life will be languid and low. And wherever the Atonement is not declared as the central glory and gladness of the Christian faith, it will haunt the background as a thing of fear, for St. Paul's judgment cannot be disputed; if righteousness come by the law then Christ died in vain; the death which is the hope and peace of the world takes rank as its worst horror and tragedy. Righteousness comes through faith in His blood, and the Church will recover her old hope and confidence when she again strikes the deep organ note of the hymn :

" Thou standest in the holiest place,
  As now for guilty sinners slain ;
  Thy blood of sprinkling speaks and prays,
  All prevalent for helpless man ;
      Thy blood is still the ransom found,
      And spreads salvation all around.

" God still respects Thy sacrifice,
  Its savour sweet does always please ;
  The offering smokes through earth and skies,
  Diffusing life and joy and peace,
      To these Thy lower courts it comes,
      And fills them with divine perfumes.

" We need not now go up to heaven
  To bring the long-sought Saviour down.
  Thou art to all that seek Thee given,
  Thou dost e'en now Thy banquet crown,
      To every faithful soul appear,
      And show Thy real presence here."

"BEING LET GO"

THE liberations of life are its crises. Some of them are as the opening of doors at which we have long beaten vainly, while others are accomplished with all the agony of sacrifice. But whether welcome or unwelcome, whether the crown of ambitions long and ardently cherished or the fulfilment of silent fears, they bring to every one, save the most thoughtless, a certain sobriety and seriousness. We feel that now we have fallen under a new order of influences, and that this may be followed by momentous catastrophes of character. Even if the first shock of change is borne well, the slow, silent attrition of time may work to a fatal end. So often a meditative heart, entering into the full fruition of desire, misses the expected happiness, seems to stand in a desolate dream, knows for the first time the real severity and trial of life.

It happens to some that their work in life has

to be changed. They have given themselves to some profession in preparation for which years have been spent—in the work of which an appreciable part of life has gone by. Through the pressure of circumstances they are forced or called out of the familiar way. It is best to be compelled to yield. When the decision is taken out of our hands, the conflicts and regrets which often try the spirit long and hardly, become impossible. When the way is not clear, it is best to abide in our lot to the end of the days. *Beware of resignations,* was the wise counsel of an experienced man. Yet to change may sometimes be the path of duty, although no outward constraint is laid upon us. In the service of Christ there is perhaps no distinction of high and low. There is a deep truth in Emerson's saying that every man is called to do somewhat unique, and no man has any other call. But the forsaking the work, the friends, the surroundings that have become accustomed and easy, is a great crisis. When the soul has to quit its whole system of things, there is, there must be, peril. "Being let go." Where shall we go? To our own company. What is our own company? Those we took sweet counsel with, and with whom we walked to the house of God? In the new world we are entering the questions that once absorbed us may sink into insignificance. We may be surrounded by associates with other ambitions, other standards. Above all, it may cease to be our interest to fight for the causes once passionately espoused. Will a new set of principles corresponding to the new interests gradually replace the old? Will it turn out that our service was no abiding devotion of the spirit? Is the future to be in disharmony with the past?

Another liberation which is a crisis comes when we are entering on easier circumstances. Poverty narrows life, but in some ways it makes it easier —less tempted, less entangled. It is the will of God that many should be "straitened" all their days, as Our Lord was "straitened." The image is that of one walking on a narrow road between two walls. He cannot deviate from the path; his easiest way is straight forward. We chafe at this, and yet the restraint may be our salvation. Nothing in human life impressed Our Lord so deeply as the alienating effects of wealth. There is the overpowering temptation to pride—a temptation fatal to all save very high and simple natures. There is the temptation to forsake old principles — a temptation which works with wonderful subtlety. A man finds that the convictions of his youth put a barrier between him and those on whose level he suddenly finds himself. He reasons that if he only were concerned he could bear it, but he cannot accept exclusion for his children. And, as Mr. Brierley recently pointed out in a striking essay, the possession of wealth brings other temptations, so that the "dangerous years" are rather in mid-life than in youth. In youth most people are held by poverty in plain, industrious, self-denying paths. When their ambition is achieved, and things grow easier, they find that the once impossible has become possible; and when the old practice of unsparing industry has been relaxed, and idle hours occur for the first time in the life, there is peril. So much is this true that wise and generous souls impose upon themselves in the hour of prosperity a noble asceticism.

We have to encounter also, as the years advance, the loss of those friends whom we cared to please, whose lives were a strong, silent pressure towards God and goodness. The chill of autumn begins to fall over us. When this is realised, when the strain of existence has to be borne alone, when year by year we sit in a longer gallery of our dead, the heart is filled with silent forebodings, with the terror of the future. There are none remaining to feed the fires of purity, and they must die. Those to whom we were bound by sweet and reverent affection have become silent, and there are none to stir the flagging powers of the spirit. We have been "let go" of the hands that detained us before the Lord, and what is to be the end?

Again, the widening of opinion is a thing which brings its own dangers. The children do not believe in all things what their fathers believed. It is not wise to desire that they should; it is better to trust bravely the increasing purpose and the widening light. But too often, when one article of the creed is abandoned, the whole is left behind. And there are many who make it their business to show that it should be so. Admit, they say, one ray of light from science and criticism, and you must cease to believe in God. We are to take no heed of such voices, from whatever quarter they come. They are the utterances of faithlessness and despair. The changes of the new knowledge have to be borne. More than that, they have to be welcomed, for in the end they will bring us good, and only good. But if a wider creed means a relaxed life, there has been no gain, but loss. We would not forget that the new light is a test of fidelity, and that in every fresh truth Christ draws near, claiming that we must not love father and mother more than Him. The peculiar temptation of these times, however, is perhaps not that. It is rather the temptation to relax hold of every Christian truth when one assumes a different aspect.

It would be easy to add to this list, and most people may do it from their own experience. It will be more profitable to ask what we are to do as the irreversible current flows on. Is the issue to be lowered temper, fading purity, secular thought and toil? When we lose the precarious secondary support, are we to lose with it also that which is primary and unfailing? Or, as the temporal and outward vanishes, are we to find ourselves armed with secret forces? Gone forth of human sympathy are we to find the divine? Does the spiritual life retire to its last retreats to die, or is it, mayhap, to fall into the arms of the eternal love? Surely the answer of the Scripture and the experience of the saints are not doubtful.

Burdened, lonely, estranged, we shall still find it gain and not loss if we receive succour from the forces that wait to be gracious. "Being let go," it will not be possible for us to over-estimate our own strength, but our very weakness is an appeal to the divine pity. Our hope, our only hope from first to last, is in the retentiveness of the divine love—in Christ's resolute hold. "We will come unto Him and make our abode with Him," is a promise great enough to meet the last extremity of our need, to encounter the most formidable enmity of circumstances. Our Lord has not forgotten how, as He moved towards the Father, He had at last to leave behind Him all human companionship. "Sit ye here while I go and pray yonder." It may come to each of us to have at last to "pray yonder." And that is the ultimate experience of life. Thence we may come back to the world and to our task assured that we are safe, knowing that it is towards Christ that our deepest thought and will and love have been tending all the while, flagging under no duty, simple and quiet in every labour, casting no shadow over the brightness of others. If the comfort of the Scriptures becomes to us thus what it would be if faith were sight, if we win the costly knowledge that spiritual support and providential guidance are the abiding realities, we may be of good cheer. For then we have overcome the world.

"THEY WITHOUT US"

"THEY without us" and with God—how do they regard us now? We know what life is to us without them. But to-night, as they sing their Evensong at the foot of the Eternal Throne, are they touched by the sense of our necessities and longings on earth? How do those who have crossed the sea of life look on their old companions who are still tossing on its stormy tide?

For answer let us remember how Christ behaved Himself when He was about to pass into the higher lands of God. He knew what awaited Him in the other world. The splendour and the peace of eternal life had been His before the world began. Did He then carry Himself as One indifferent to those He was leaving, as One who was to forget them and content Himself in a higher fellowship? Behold, how He loved them! As He gazed out into the glory of the Father, His thought was still for them. Beneath the magic significant night, silent with excess of meaning, He said, " In my Father's house are many mansions; I go to prepare a place for you." He asked to be remembered, and He promised to return : " This do in remembrance of me. . . . Ye do show the Lord's death till He come." If Christ on the steps of the throne dearly prized the remembrance of those He left behind, if Christ's concern with the world did not end with His dying, did not end even with His ascension, surely the same is true of those who had no life before this, to whom heaven was a strange place, who bore into it no loves except those which began on earth.

Phillips Brooks has said that the haunting fear of the disciples during the days of our Lord's flesh must have been that He would leave them. Two friends begin life together. They sit side by side at the village school, on the college bench, and in due time they go out into the world. A few years, and one has greatly distanced the other. He has shown more various powers, greater energy, quicker apprehension. His mind has become familiar with the regions of which his old companion knows nothing. The ancient friendship may be kept up, but an element of pain has entered it. One feels that his friend has passed into other experiences, has gone whither he cannot come. In other words, his friend has left him in the spirit, if not outwardly. Of two comrades, one discovers the glory of Christ, the other remains in blindness, and the two spirits cannot again enter into free and rich communion. Christ, as the disciples saw, was rising higher. The interval between Him and them seemed to widen. Near as He might be, there was an infinite separateness which fell ever and anon on all their relations. There was a fear which He was at last to confirm, that He would depart from this mortal life, and that His visible presence would vanish from their eyes. The last distress was but the culmination of many misgivings that had gone before it. The disciples kept thinking that they were not love-worthy, that Christ, who knew them, who was so far above them, could not be touched by any abiding affection for men so ignorant, so sinful, so weak as they.

This was because they did not understand the meaning of love. A thoughtful writer has said that one of the last lessons life teaches is the difference between love and admiration. At first we believe that they are the same, and think that we prize love when we are really exulting in admiration. But heaven is the world of love, not the world of admiration. The disciples rejoiced when men admired them, when the spirits were subject unto them. At the outset of His work, Jesus Himself was tempted to accept admiration at the cost of love. He rejected it, and had to make the most of such love as was given Him, for of admiration He had very little from His puzzled and stammering followers. Indeed, as the same writer remarks, love is hard to express; one must master half a dozen languages besides that of the tongue before he can render it. Admiration is a pungent, concentrated, unmistakable thing, and men drink it in as the elixir of life. Doubtless, when admiration is sincere, it elevates those who give it, and it may greatly help and quicken those who receive it. It is the starved heart that does not know what it is generously to admire. Multitudes of men and women would have acquitted themselves more worthily if they had received at the right time the encouragement they had earned. Still, admiration will not compare with love. Admiration at the best takes hold of something which is not the essence of the soul. Admiration is based too often on the power to do brilliant things. Admiration may have even a lower foundation than that; it may rise or fall with the appreciation of the world. So long as a man succeeds, it follows him. Whenever he appears to fail, even though the apparent failure may be an actual triumph, it turns away in disappointment. Love does not depend on anything external; love does not ask the opinion of others; love lays hold of the heart and clings to it. It attaches itself to what endures, rejoices, not that the spirits are subject to the dear ones, but rather is glad because their names are written in heaven. "Love beareth all things, believeth all things, hopeth all things, endureth all things." Love can survive straining and bruising; admiration is brittle. Admiration replaces one ideal very easily by another. Love cannot forget. It holds the door open for new-comers, but it lets no guest pass out. Admiration is the spectator that turns away when its eyes are feasted. Love is the communicant at the table of a perpetual sacrament.

Now the misgiving of the disciples was due in part at least to this confusion between admiration and love. Very likely when Jesus chose them, they imagined that He saw something in them the world had missed, that He admired some gift of force, or eloquence, or courage, or wisdom. As the parting hour drew near, this illusion wholly vanished. They saw that He was infinitely above them. The one possible consolation was that He loved them, that He would not cease, that He could not cease, loving them wherever He went. The whole burden of His sacred farewell was an assurance of this. He expounded to them the deep mystery of love, constant for evermore. He told them that true love was union, that by union His people were part of Himself, that seeing they were knit to Him they must follow Him wherever He went. He was to rise higher, but He rose to raise them. The forces of His heavenly power were to be spent for this, and He could not see of the travail of His soul and be satisfied till the Church was with Him in glory. So we know that the last, the least, the weakest, is awaited at the fountains of life.

Now we can answer our question, and silence our misgiving. "They without us shall not be made perfect"; "they without us" could not, if we might dare to say it, be made perfect even by the love of God. The perfection of the blessed dead cannot be achieved till the living they wait for come. We feel that we are not worthy now to loose their shoe-latchet, or to touch their garments' hem; but since love is love, that must not trouble us. While they complete themselves in regions beyond our view, we are to remember them, to look for them, to prepare for them. We must try to keep the straight path, so far as we can see it, to seek that we may reach the spirit-land unsoiled and noble. They remember us, they wait for us, they will welcome us. They are saying, if we had ears to hear, "Dearly beloved and longed for, my joy and crown, so stand fast in the Lord, my dearly beloved."

THE WEIGHT OF THE ENDS OF THE WORLD

WRITING to the Corinthians, St. Paul recalls the experiences of the fathers, and tells us that these things were written for our admonition upon whom the ends of the world are come. Writing to the Romans, he says more fully, "Whatsoever things were written aforetime were written for our learning, that we, through patience and comfort of the Scriptures, might have hope." We are conscious, as the first believers were, of the weight of the ends of the world. The century draws to its close, and men are oppressed by an unwonted burden. The buoyant enthusiasm of the years not very far distant, when it seemed as if the kingdoms of the world were to go under and become the one kingdom of the Lamb, has passed away. Apathy is the order of things in every sphere. Enthusiasms fail and flag, and even the faithful question why so little has come of schemes into which much heart has been thrown, and for which great sacrifices have been made. Of course there is true gain, though little pleasure, in getting rid of the false enthusiasms and misleading hallucinations of youth. But to have passed through vast tracts of thought and feeling and effort, and to realise at the end of them that the current is against us, to feel in its terrible force the temptation to give all up, to drift with the tide of opinion, and to end as the champions and apologists of what our best years were spent in rebuking and withstanding—this indeed is bitter. Ours is, books like Max Nordau's tell us, a time of feverish restlessness and blunted discouragement. Nordau describes very well the *fin de siècle* sentiment as a practical emancipation from traditional disciplines which theoretically are still in force. It seems as if the higher aspirations of life were stinted and cramped, as if cold water were thrown upon noble and burning impulses, as if the wisdom of years were won only to mislead and chill, as if high and severe views of duty were but morbid states of conscience, in due time to be outlived.

Nordau says, truly enough, that it is ridiculous to attach importance to the end of a century in itself. A century is not a living being, born like a beast or a man, passing through all the stages of existence, gradually ageing and declining after blooming childhood, joyous youth, and vigorous maturity, to die with the expiration of the hundredth year, after being afflicted in its last decade with all the infirmities of mournful senility. As he reminds us, the division of time is not identical among civilised beings. The Mohammedans are reckoning their fourteenth century, and the Jews their fifteenth century, while every day a hundred and thirty thousand human beings are born for whom the world begins with that same day. Still, he is wrong, perhaps, in saying that the *fin de siècle* tendency rises from the habit of the human mind to project externally its own subjective states. There is more than this. At certain periods we strike a balance; we are conscious of a transition; we reckon our gains and losses, and it is but too likely that the results may disappoint us even before we have settled accounts. There are forebodings that make the heart sink and unnerve the hand. The harvest falls far short of our hopes, and we cannot summon any true confidence about the future before us. The early Christians had something of the same feeling. As the years wore on they, too, felt as if every tradition were rending, and as if to-morrow would not link itself with to-day. In other words, it is to the *fin de siècle* feeling that St. Paul addresses himself.

In such a world, and at such an hour, the Apostle tells us, we are left with the Holy Scriptures.

He reminds us, indeed, of the necessity and the majesty of patience. Those to whom he spoke, as he speaks to us, had seen much of life's actual weariness, pettiness, failures, insignificance, but they had seen also, else they were sadly blind, something of its wonders, its surprises, its victories. Even a secular wisdom has warned us against a too easy despair. Even folly, as in the German song, has the same lesson.

> " It will go better yet—it will go better yet!
> The world it is round, and will roll if 'tis let!
> 'Tis the word of a fool! but the word it is true;
> And if you be wise, you will think so too.
> It will go better yet—it will go better yet!
> The world it is round, and will roll if 'tis let!
>
> This sighing, and moaning, and raging, and raving
> But adds pain to pain, and new griefs to your grieving.

> Oh! shake not and shrink not in ill—look above!
> Time changes and changes wherever you rove.
>
> It will go better yet—it will go better yet!
> The world it is round, and will roll if 'tis let!
> It will go better yet—it will go better yet!
> The world it is round, and will roll if 'tis let!
> 'Tis the word of a fool! but the word it is true.
> *And if you be wise, you will think so too."*

Time, in the poet's words, brings roses, and the loveliest of them all is the white rose of death. But our true, abiding rest, our unfailing comfort, is to be found in the sacred Scriptures. Open them, and if we will we may escape from the currents and waves of the atmosphere around us, and be plunged in the profoundest sense of the presence of God.

We take the word in the larger sense, and include the full revelation of Christ. There is a tendency to talk as if critical research had somehow made the Bible less necessary, less final than it was wont to be. We venture to say that as time goes on it will be more and more clearly seen that the Bible is the one essential book. Ewald, in that characterisation of the Bible in which he seems to have ultimately rested, says that the Bible, and the Bible alone, is the mirror in which we can read of the conditions and stages of the perfect, true religion which is necessary for all future generations of men. Robertson Smith, another believing critic, says that it is from the Bible only that we learn how the one purpose of history is the purpose of everlasting love worked out in and through human personality by a personal redeeming God. Not only so. Whatever religious thought has done, there is one thing for which, after trial enough, it has proved incompetent; it has not added a sentence to the New Testament. That closes where it closed at first.

We commence then by saying that always the true beginning of the higher life and its divine support are to be found in the word of God, and there alone. As Our Lord has told us, the seed is the Word of God. The Word of God reveals the thought of God about Himself and His purpose for the race. By the Word of the Lord were the heavens made, and by the same Word is the divine life in man created, nourished, and defended. Though every other religious book disappeared from the face of the earth, though the thoughts, the prayers, the communion, the triumph, and the tears of the saints were lost to us, we should still have everything necessary for the maintenance and enrichment of the divine society if the Bible were left to us. With it alone the Church would know all that it knows to-day, or rather, we should say, would have in possession all true knowledge, however much or little of it had been grasped. This truth bears significantly on many present tendencies. Even believing preachers often try to gather the people with words of man. They survey the careers of heroes and saints, they discuss political and social problems of the time, and in various ways attempt to interest and impress their audiences. But unless the preacher interests people in what God has said, he has done nothing. Unless he impresses his hearers by what God has said, he has not begun his work. Though he were to attract a multitude, and move them by the contagious influence of his own earnestness, he would have made no advance towards the beginning of the Christian life. Only when he is able to tell men what God has said, does he begin to sow the true seed. If he sows the Word of God, he will never be unhopeful, he will be in the large world of comfort, and peace, and strength which God Himself inhabits, and the phenomena of the hour will be seen in their true transiency. "The grass withereth, the flower thereof fadeth away, but the Word of the Lord endureth for ever." And this is the Word which by the Gospel is preached unto men.

Let us try to put the same truth in another form. We have tried, many of us, by strenuous effort and discipline to find God. It seemed to us as if God were distant, and as if by our own painful searchings and journeyings we might find Him. But it is He who calls for us, who speaks in the righteousness and pity of His holy Word, ere ever we call for Him. The divine life, it has been said nobly, begins when *we* answer the cry of God, not when God answers ours. When He speaks to us, we are past the doubtings and the perplexities which break and crush the heart. We know. We rest in the work that was finished by the dying Christ, we rely on the will, and the thought, and the love of the Eternal. Our life flourishes, for it has for its deep root no conclusion of the human intellect, no resolution of the human will, but the truth and will of God.

Once more, we exaggerate our petty share in

the divine work of redemption. We think that the Church would stand still if our task was not performed rightly. We groan and fret as if the whole burden of the future course of God's cause among men rested on our bowed shoulders. But it is He who has in charge the world which He loved so well that He gave His Son to die for it, and the Church which He purchased with His own blood. The new life that is in the world has its origin above the sphere of history. The prophetic teaching, as Robertson Smith says, proved by its operation on history to be what it professed to be—no mere natural efflux of the past history and past development of the people, but a new and living power, the utterance of a new life, which because it is a new life could spring only from the infinite source of all life. When He to whom all prophecy points appeared in the fulness of time, the saving self-manifestation of God was completed. Thus we know that though the divine work of redemption has not been a steady advance, though the course of the Christian Church has not been always upwards and onwards, but sometimes downwards and backwards, yet there has been no interregnum. There is no interregnum now. The Lord reigneth. We are to do our utmost, and yet to be sure that though we are needed by God, we are not necessary to God; God wants us, but God can do without us. Our work is to be done with a peaceful and high heart. If we keep ourselves to the Word of God, we shall in time have imparted to us something of its divine serenity. Why should we not rise to the calmness of an Apostle's thought? We talk of the trend of things, of the irresistible drift of opinion, where St. Paul would have quietly spoken of the "spirit that now worketh in the children of disobedience." About the great future we may be confident, even though the little future is dark to us, and even though attempts to penetrate it may seem like straining the eyes at nightfall over the edge of a precipice.

THE BACKWATER OF LIFE

A NOTEWORTHY article was published lately by Mr. James Payn. The keynote is struck in the first sentence: "It is a strange feeling to one who has been immersed in affairs, and as it were in the mid-stream of what we call life, to find oneself in its backwater, crippled and helpless, but still able to see through the osiers on the island between us what is passing along the river, the passenger vessels, and the pleasure boats, and to hear faintly the voices, and the laughter, and the strong language mellowed by distance from the slow-moving barges." He goes on to speak of the bitter sense of humiliation which comes from being reduced to dependence upon others. True, one is made to know the immeasurable goodness of humanity, but those in the backwater have no means of showing the gratitude with which they are filled.

They think—and this seems to be the special pang—of the blessedness of the past, when they were too happy to be aware of their happiness. The delights of love and labour are forbidden them, and dead, unhappy nights usher in weary days all empty of delight. "'Oh, Lord, how long?' is then our bitter cry." The paper closes with the words: "One of the saddest conditions to which the human mind can be reduced, not from faith, but from pain and weariness, is no longer to fear the shadow feared of man." This cry of unfeigned anguish will arrest attention, and will especially move those whom for many years Mr. Payn has charmed by his wisdom, his kindliness, and his wit. There is nothing weak in his complaint; it is a sad, hopeless, magnanimous confession that he has made to the world. He has never been effusive, never wont to break wantonly the silence that should shroud the heart. With all his frankness, he has habitually maintained the scrupulous and delicate seclusion of self-respecting men. We have always known him to be full of emotion, his vivacity has never been hard, and his wit has never been merciless. Sometimes, but very rarely, he has shown us glimpses of his deeper nature, as in the pathetic lines where he questions how long that pause of mournfulest silence, which comes when the doors have closed behind us, will last. But as a rule, he has posed as a gay and cheerful stoic, and it must be owned that the rags of stoicism, threadbare though they be, have covered truly noble natures in these days, as in the time of the Antonines. But here his stoicism breaks down hopelessly before the facts of life.

Mr. Payn's complaint of life's close chimes in with a prevailing feeling. It would not be too much to say that sententious wisdom and sentimental poetry combine in disparaging the final years. "That powerful distemper old age," as Montaigne has it, is universally looked upon as at best bringing us to flat and dull experiences, a period of disappointment, failure, and flagging life, full of losses that find no compensation. It is useless to say in reply that the passing of youthful ardour is made up for by experience, by liberty, by the influence which years bring. Especially is it useless when youth has been brilliant and glorified. Nothing then seems to atone for the flight of the passionate and exciting years. Nowadays, when the tendency is so decidedly towards the enriching of early life, it is inevitable that the later period should seem to many poor in comparison. Readers of Horace Walpole will remember his lugubrious forebodings when he was only between forty and fifty. He wrote: "Do not think it is pain that makes me give this low-spirited air to my letter. No! it is the prospect of what is to come, and the sensation of what is passing, that affects me. The loss of youth is melancholy enough, but to enter into old age through the gate of infirmity is most disheartening." At sixty-six he described himself as a ruin, and the gloom steadily advanced for the fourteen years more left to him. We constantly hear the fret and moan of dissatisfaction that youth has gone. The observed of all observers may even come to shrink with shame from the notice they once courted.

> "Shall I believe him ashamed to be seen?
> For only once in the village street,
> Last year, I caught a glimpse of his face,
> A grey old wolf and lean."

We bethink ourselves with a thrill of wonder that Mr. Payn's "backwater of life" is John Bunyan's land of Beulah. It is there, when mortal strength is spent and the earthly life almost run out, that the pilgrims "have more rejoicing than in parts more remote from the kingdom to which they are bound." The dreamer is very bold. For Christians themselves it is hard to believe that the days before death may be the radiant crown of earthly existence, filled with the triumph and the peace of heaven. This is the ultimate glory of Christian experience, and it rests daily on lives where the powers of the world to come visibly counteract and reverse the forces of time and nature. Is it so, that as life lingers out to its last moment amid the wreck of all things, as the air echoes dully with the sound of lamentation, as death after death falls heavily on the heart, a new lustre may fall on the fading years? Is it so, that the dry rod may bud and blossom, and that at the moment of withering a new life may rush in through all the arid fibres? Even so if the law of the spirit of life in Christ Jesus sets us free from the law of sin and death.

But we are willing to argue upon lower ground. It is one of the most familiar and certain of experiences that faith brightens the otherwise darkened days of life. We will not speak of the wonderful heroism with which hopeless, incurable agony is often borne, and that by tender and shrinking souls. But there is a generous submission to helplessness, to being served, which we have often thought reveals patience, tenderness, purity, and religion at their highest. For it is part of the Christian's training to be willing to receive sympathy as well as to give it. Men and women who are full of care and service for others often keep a proud silence on their own grief. Yet the Christian way would be to tell it, for the Christian should recognise that the deepest and most lasting joy is in giving rather than in receiving.

Some readers will remember how, when Miss Bremer's character, "Ma chère Mère," is dying, and her devoted servant, Elsa, is advised to be comforted by the thought of her beloved mistress in heaven, she says, "But what shall I do without her? And then she must have somebody in heaven to wait upon her, and be at her side night and day." "She will be with the angels then, Elsa." "Ah! dear madam, they could not conform to her temper as I can. They have not lived with her for forty years." The principle can be carried much higher, so high that we do not hesitate to say that willingness to be ministered to may in certain cases be the most touching and perfect form of self-abnegation.

Nor do Christians fear to recall the joys behind them. They shut the door softly on the gladness that is over, and look forward. No chill need fall on the happy hours—they will be our own again. Christ Himself had His "No more," but all the sadness went as He thought of re-union. "I will not drink henceforth of this fruit of the vine till I drink it new with you in my Father's kingdom." So the Christian "No more" is only till "the day in the kingdom of God."

Again, Christianity will help us to meet enforced inaction. It will help us more easily, no doubt, if we have laboured while we could. Then we can reflect in the long, passive hours that "of toil and moil the day was full." Even if the cherished work has been forbidden, if it has been hardly begun, or not begun at all, the depression of failure may very well be banished by the thought of an undying life in God. After all, we are never old till we feel old, and nobody feels old until he feels that his work is done. So long as there is in us some faculty hidden from daylight, some capacity still unrevealed, some work still to accomplish, we are young, and faith looks to the future life as the development and completion of this. The night taper, says one, burns long enough if it lets in the Eternal Day. There may be, there doubtless is, a momentary pang in surrendering some kinds of work to which we thought ourselves specially elected, and yet in these things also God is worthy of our trust. Perhaps there is no such unspeakably pathetic resignation as that of a mother parting from her children. And yet every day with what victorious faith is this care cast upon God! Schiller, on his premature deathbed, kissed and blessed his youngest child of seven months old, and gazed at the helpless creature with yearning tenderness. Yet a little later, when they asked him how he felt, he said, "Calmer and calmer." Is there any better preparation for life and death than that of the girded loins and the burning lamp?

THE SCHOOL OF TYRANNUS

AS Dr. Liddon points out in his "Clerical Life and Work," the great opportunity of St. Paul's life was perhaps his teaching for two years in the school of Tyrannus at Ephesus. The Apostle himself describes it as "a great and effectual door." Its claims were so urgent that they kept him at Ephesus when a great moral struggle was going on at Corinth, and his sentence was imperatively demanded. He had been preaching at Ephesus, first in the synagogue, where he was denounced in terms of insult. Then he and his gathered in one of the lounges attached to the gymnasiums and public baths in the city, which was frequented by Tyrannus, probably a teacher of rhetoric. There for two years he preached every day, with results that affected deeply both Jewish and pagan society. Dr. Liddon remarks suggestively, "Every ministerial life has such opportunities sooner or later. We may work for some years amidst the discouragements of the synagogue, but the school of Tyrannus comes at last."

"The school of Tyrannus comes at last." This holds true of public workers in every sphere. Those who set their thoughts high at the beginning come in the end to their desire. There is a point at which life spreads out and comes to larger things. A sun-burst falls on the road. The days grow full and rich. They are undisturbed by misfortune, reverse, and foreboding. The preacher who has a gift for his work sooner or later has a chance of showing it. He gains the ear of the people, and is set in a conspicuous place. He is able to hold and conquer men's minds. There is a living interest in him and his proclamations. This period may pass by. Few men maintain themselves on the high tableland of uniform prosperity for many years. When their life is summed up, it is easy to point out and to limit the period of shining success.

The same truth, of course, applies equally to the statesman, the artist, the author. There are few more pathetic chapters in biography than the story of Sir Walter Scott's sad, heroic struggle against disease and decay. He lived for many years in the broad sunshine. His prosperity was too great to last, too equal, too complete, too unchequered. At last something came to "tame the glaring white" of that splendour. One by one the gifts of fortune were withdrawn. The brave old man calmly saw them vanish, till last of all his magic wand was broken. But he could hardly realise that his imagination no longer kindled to the old heat, that the spell was beginning to fail him. "I have lost, it is plain, the power of interesting the country, and ought in justice to all parties to retire while I have some credit; but this is an important step, and I will not be obstinate about it if it be necessary." Lesser men have in their degree the same experience. With infinite reluctance they begin to note painfully that their books excite less and less interest, that the disappointed eyes of their old readers are turning away from them. New stars are rising, and the old are disappearing. So far as these public experiences are concerned, outsiders see the end of the golden hour much more quickly than those who have lived it. But even for them it becomes vain to struggle against the conviction that the sunlight is over, and that henceforth the path must slope downwards.

Nearly all of us, even the humblest, have in our own lives a time which, as we look back upon it, we know to have been blessed and warmed by love as no time can be again. There were calm years when the home circle was unbroken, when the longings of the heart were answered. Days succeed, it may be, in which we are tossed from pain to pain. Even if the heartache is deadened and the life finds an outlet in other interests, there is still the memory of the past and those who peopled it,

> "Whose comin' step there's ears that won't,
> No, not lifelong, leave off awaitin'."

The Antiquary with his packet of letters marked *Eheu Evelina;* Mr. Gilfil in the "Scenes of Clerical Life," are types of what exists under the most unlikely exteriors.

Looking back upon such times, after they are irrevocably over, and after something has been learned by actual experience of life and labour and death, our wonder is that they gladdened us so little. It seems incredible that these days, now thought of with such yearning, should have seemed common and tame while they passed. Yet perhaps few can say that they prized as they should have done the opportunity that was given them. They took for granted what they had, and looked on to a more abundant future. They suffered small things to break their peace. They were not aware, as they should have been, of the goodness of God and man. These lines will be read by many who, as they read them, have greater means of happiness and usefulness than they will ever have again. Let them prize their good things, and yet not prize them overmuch. Perhaps, when we have left the school of Tyrannus behind, we shall perceive that our work in it might have been done better. Many preachers, many authors, lose their audience because they yield to vanity and sloth. So their hour passes never to return. But oftener, perhaps, the end comes in the providence of God. The message has been delivered, and there is no more to say. If this is our case, let us be thankful that our day was given us and that our work has been done. Let us descend without repining, and give over our place to others. Those who are still in the noontide of opportunity should not wait for trouble and failure to teach them sympathy with defeated men. Too often, when things are well with us, we refuse to see the importunate faces that look through the silken curtains. We think we can walk sure and strong and steady on the heights, that we know how to abound. Influence stays longest with those who use it gently, whose power walks hand in hand with tenderness, patience, consideration. There are many who, like Cordelia, love and are silent. A day will come when they would give the world if they could say the words that might be spoken now.

When the school of Tyrannus is left behind, and we settle down to obscure labour, daily becoming more obscure and feeble, when life grows solitary, let us not too much regret what has gone from us. The heart should not be disturbed, but deepened by the thought that the past is past. It was ours. We have had our day and lived our life. There is still service to render; and true love knows no struggle of great and little. What was best in the past is ours more than it ever was. Wordsworth's lovely poem on his last meeting with Scott is inspired by the Christian temper:

> "No public and no private care
>   The free-born mind enthralling,
> We made a day of happy hours
>   Our happy days recalling.
> And if as Yarrow, through the woods
>   And down the meadow ranging,
> Did meet us with unaltered face,
>   Though we were changed and chang ng,
>
> If then some natural shadow spread
>   The inward prospect over,
> The soul's deep valley was not slow
>   Its brightness to recover.
> Ah no, the visions of the past
>   Sustained the heart in feeling,
> Life as she is—our changeful Life,
>   With friends and kindred dealing."

Besides, we are to look, not backward nor downward, but onward. The best is before us. Whatever has been forfeited or misprized, our hearts are to be filled with a splendid and exalting hope. Not far from us are the new heavens and the new earth. This life at its highest has the glory of the star, and we pass to the glory of the sun.

In that He saith, A new earth, He hath made the first old.

THE MOTHERS OF ST. PAUL

IN his Epistle to the Romans St. Paul salutes "Rufus, chosen in the Lord, and his mother and mine." In his Epistle to the Galatians he applies the cherished name to that heavenly Jerusalem towards which the tides of his heart were set. "Jerusalem which is above is free, which is the mother of us all." Life *im Ganzen*, it has been said, is the life of one for whom over and over again what was once precious has become indifferent. For St. Paul this happened once and for ever in the hour when he saw the face of Christ and heard His voice from heaven.

The Apostle's life was rooted and grounded in love, and, indeed, we hear more of love in his epistles than in the Gospels. Love to him was of the spirit, rather than of the earth and the senses. The love that mastered and filled him was primarily the love of Christ. From the day when Christ called him, he was carried out to sea on that great wave, and he could not return upon his former thoughts or resist the constant current which drove him onward. That wave was never spent. The returning tide never cast him upon the shore. To the last the creating word of St. Paul's universe was love. It was life's crown to love and to be loved, and the Apostle, elect in Christ, was ever stretching forth the hand of redemption and blessing. Everywhere the great, astounding, overwhelming fact that smote him in the face was that men did not know this love of Christ, or knowing it refused it. Yet he is silent as to much. We may almost say that he ignores human love in its deepest, most miraculous, most revealing sense. Of course he had no room in his redeemed nature for mere passion—the handful of dry heather, as it has been called, which is set on fire and cast into the waters of death. George Meredith has rightly marked the one false note in Mr. Myers's great poem, a note struck in partial forgetfulness of this. And so far as we know the great enchantment was lacking to his cup, that human devotion to which the solemn and sacred name of love is best applied. And yet we cannot tell what lava there might have been under the snow. We cannot gaze on the

Apostle's inner life. He did not wear his heart on his sleeve, and none may know what names were graven there, names that never crossed his lips, names that were part of the sweet and dreadful past, names sunk into dim and deep abysses whence no hand could pluck them forth.

What we do know is that his love was mainly a paternal love. As Jowett says, there was in his heart "an affection which seems to be as strong and as individual towards all mankind as other men are capable of feeling towards a single person." St. Paul evermore beheld the world of suffering beneath and beside the world of joy, the innumerable multitude of the wretched, the forgotten, the lonely, benumbed by their long despair. His place was with them. His portion was their tears and toil. His affection was serious, patient, deliberate as that of a heart touched to its core by the universal woe in its length and breadth and height. He was as one to whom the world was a great hospital and himself an unwearied nurse by the bedside of the patients. He strove to heal the wounds that from generation to generation remained unclosed, and he met each emergency as it arose with the calm wisdom which comes to saintly souls who have explored all and have looked at the worst in the light of reconciling love. He carried in his heart that inward Presence which was one day to be revealed. He saw the fires of love rising up from under the soil in the midst of a frozen world. He was willing to be accursed from Christ for his brethren, his kinsmen according to the flesh. Before him life spread as a great shipwreck. Existence was made up of pain. Men and women wore the burning crown. He possessed the secret, the anodyne that would turn the racking agony into peace, and wherever men needed healing or wherever the healed needed to be taught patience and strength, he was busy—bearing upon him the care of all the churches, coming out in every trouble with all his faculties roused and stimulated, knowing what to say and what to do, as a mother by some divine instinct knows by the bedside of her ailing child. It was typical of his life that he stood forth in the doomed ship in Adria, in the darkness and despair of the tempest, to take command and speak the word of heartening and hope.

It is thus very moving and significant that he sometimes felt the need of being mothered and found that need supplied. In the absence of human sympathy, he seemed sometimes almost to lose the power of action. And human sympathy came in its sweetest form when it asked little and gave all, when it comforted and cherished the weary, burdened Apostle and brought back to him the security and restfulness and peace of childhood. First of all, he found this comfort in a nameless woman, the mother of Rufus. Of Rufus we know very little, perhaps nothing. But there is some reason to believe that he was of Nero's household, one of St. Paul's converts and friends in Asia and Eastern Europe, who entered it after conversion as purchased slaves or otherwise. The mother of Rufus, who was also the mother of St. Paul, was thus probably obscure and humble. But in the great school where all Zion's children are taught of God and where nothing avails but the illumination of the Holy Ghost vouchsafed to the obedient heart, she was among the foremost. Her life was doubtless closely limited in one sense. But it was not limited on the side of the ideal. She built for her dark poverty a house not made with hands, and St. Paul shared gladly and thankfully the shelter of its roof. Wordsworth has pictured in various places kind, great, motherly hearts among the poor, nowhere perhaps more effectively than in his poem, "The Old Cumberland Beggar":

> "Man is dear to man; the poorest poor
> Long for some moments in a weary life
> When they can know and feel that they have been,
> Themselves, the fathers and the dealers-out
> Of some small blessings; have been kind to such
> As needed kindness, for this single cause,
> That we have all of us one human heart.
> Such pleasure is to one kind Being known,
> My neighbour, when with punctual care, each week
> Duly as Friday comes, though pressed herself
> By her own wants, she from her store of meal
> Takes one unsparing handful for the scrip
> Of this old Mendicant, and, from her door
> Returning with exhilarated heart,
> Sits by her fire, and builds her hope in heaven."

So St. Paul and his mother built their hope in the Heavenly City which was the mother of both, which is the mother of us all.

We can well conceive how the thought of the mother city comforted and strengthened the Apostle as the years ran out. Existence to him was always bounded and overspread by the Jerusalem which is above. His life was not a journey on and on over the barren moor, with no prospect before him but the waste and the sundown. Jerusalem, stable, motherly, holy, was the end of his pilgrimage. She grew dearer and kinder with the passing of the days. Some whom he loved were in Christ before him. Many were in Jerusalem before him. What was strange to the Apostle, it has been well said, was not the invisible, but the visible, not the life of the spirit, but the life of the flesh. That life was death, and what ensphered it was not reality, but phantom. To him, as to all believing souls, the thought of death came often, even in the midst of life and labour, with a rush of home-sickness. We can see it in this very Epistle to the Galatians, where he braces himself to the task of dispute, and yet protests that his last word has been said, and that he is not to be troubled from thenceforth, because he bears the absolving marks of Christ. So we can conceive what was passing when the hour of his release arrived. To the eye of the world his career ended in desertion, failure, collapse. But as the old man was led along the Ostian way to die, his mother Jerusalem bent over him with rapturous welcome. He saw those who had gone before, the martyrs in their robes of crimson and the saints in white. Life behind him was like a far-off storm at sea. He was filled with a sense of everlasting triumph as he neared the high world he had longed to dwell in, that world whose air was home. The city of God is glad, and her gladness transfigured him. He saw the earthly vanish and himself entering into the fellowship whereof all the love we know is but a trembling shadow, that city where all we love is restored. To the eye of sense his career ended as forlornly and lovelessly as might be. To the eye of faith his death was the rising of his mother to take her wearied child to her breast.

FROM GLORY TO GLORY

IF we were asked at the beginning of a year to describe the course of life, we might be slow to give for answer our very inmost thought. And if we did, the response might run, "From weakness to weakness, from failure to failure, from humiliation to humiliation," or even it might be "From shame to shame." How wonderful appears the picture of St. Paul, who describes the believing life as a passage "from glory to glory"! In the epistle where these words occur the Apostle shows himself acutely conscious of life's miseries, privations, and agonies. He was then suffering from troubles whose pressure had almost exhausted his strength. He describes himself as nameless, poor, sorrowful, and dying. He understood as well as any of us what it is to feel that the romance of life has faded, that the country of youth has been left behind, that there is nothing one can do but bewail the irrecoverable sweetness of the past. Yet his spirit rises unsubdued from the griefs and wrecks of time, and he speaks as one of the great company who, "beholding as in a glass the glory of the Lord, are changed into the same image from glory to glory, even as by the Spirit of the Lord." For let it be noted that he was not speaking of himself alone. Else we might have said, "This may be true for such an one as St. Paul, advancing through all those years without one backward look or one yielding thought. But how can it be true of us who are so weary of the incessant struggle, and whose hopes cannot rise from unlooked-for and merciless strokes?" The answer is that to those who see truly the course of every redeemed life moves forward to its perfect consummation.

In the first place St. Paul affirms that life to the believer is a glory. The whole current of modern thought runs against this estimate. At most it may be admitted that life in certain conditions is a more or less happy delusion. Even so much as this will scarcely be granted in these years of the dying century, when pessimism is eating out the very heart of our literature and is gradually taking possession of the general mind. How far we have travelled in the days between Charles Dickens and Thomas Hardy! One may say without irreverence and with perfect truth that to Dickens the Blessed Trinity was practically identical with an omnipotent firm of Cheeryble Brothers. To him the administration of the universe was benevolent, benevolent in the sentimental fashion of "A Christmas Carol." Mr. Hardy's whole philosophy and religion are summed up in the infinitely bitter words, "The President of the Immortals had finished his sport with Tess." Open as "Jude the Obscure" is to many criticisms, we cannot agree with those who take it simply as an attack on marriage. It is much rather an effort to show that the universe and mankind are deliberately organised for misery. Let human beings do what they will, let them marry or abstain from marriage, and they will still be wretched. The loftier the ideals that rise before them, the more ardently they endeavour to pursue them, the more absolute will their failure be and their consequent agony. We need not wonder at this. It is nothing but what must happen as the world breaks loose from God. Unless life is divine with the love of Christ, it must be sunless. St. Paul was profoundly sensible of the sin and the misery of mankind. After nearly two thousand years more of sorrowful human history, no fact or experience has come to light that would have taken the Apostle by surprise. But to him the vastness of sin, the vastness of pain, were not the first and overpowering facts. He knew that which was greater than them all. He was lost in the immensities of the love of Christ, the love that signified its strength on Calvary, the love whose length and breadth and depth and height far transcended knowledge. Life to St. Paul was a glory because it had been redeemed by the precious blood, and was wrapt round by the divine charity. True, its inexorable facts remain. But they are wholly transfigured. For the veil has been undone for ever, and with open face we behold Christ. On our poor house the rains may descend and the winds blow, but it may be nevertheless the palace of the great King. Life may go out wretchedly and solitarily, in a garret, in a workhouse, and yet to the eye of faith the promise of Christ may be kept, "I will come again and receive you unto myself."

More difficult even for Christians is the next thought, that life is a growing glory. After a certain period, we come to shrink from change, and yet, as has often been said, Christianity welcomes change. It takes " new " for one of its favourite words. It keeps speaking of a new covenant, new creatures, a new name, and new heavens. It encourages us to go forward, to grow tired of poor conditions, and to press against limits. Instead of fearing a change in our circumstances, we should rather welcome it. But some—perhaps not many—of those who read these lines will keep thinking that a change has come over themselves, a change which they fear, and which they can hardly understand. It may be that this is the result—it is so most frequently—of some blow struck straight and deep at the roots of happiness.

We no longer hear much about the doctrine of transmigration, the doctrine which was Henry More's golden key to the mystery of the universe. Perhaps we can hardly follow the arguments by which it is supported. But when an appeal is made to the latent elements that underlie our present consciousness, and when it is maintained that there is a hidden world in which the subterranean river of personality flows, it is not difficult after certain experiences to understand what is meant. For does it not seem sometimes as if a new spirit had taken possession of the existing body, when the true soul has departed? Many people live until they die, but many people do not. In Mrs. Oliphant's powerful novel "Agnes," there is the most vivid expression of this fact that we know of in literature. The vitality that survives so much is at last mastered and disappears. Illness does not come, death does not come, duties continue to present themselves and are laboriously discharged. But life, so far as it is a matter of personal desire, satisfaction, and actual being, has ceased and stopped short. The sufferers feel that they have had their day, and yet much may remain of the hard tale of years which God sometimes exacts to the last moment from those of His creatures to whom He has given strength to endure. The new spirit that inhabits the form may be angel or demon, or it may be a most human spirit, but it is a substitute even though no one may be aware of the substitution. The life it was pleasure to possess and happiness to continue has been broken short off and has come to an end. What are we to say in the face of facts like these? How can it be that such transmutations are a passage from glory to glory? For answer we may reply that time must do its work. "How deep and awful," says one, "are the wounds that time and truth can heal!" How often wild, dark sorrows show themselves at last the fair, enlightened work of God. The heart may be wondrously revived and quieted, and a new happiness may link itself with the old. But this cannot always be. St. Paul himself spoke not much of what lay before him in his earthly course. He earnestly desired to be clothed upon with his house from heaven. Then we must say that in God is the continuous thread of all our years. Then we must boldly rest in the faith that there is a life in God which furnishes its own health, its own wealth, its own good. The whole discipline of Providence is bent towards our securing and perfecting that secret immortal life. It may seem as if the heart were rifled and broken by the harshnesses and the amazements of its way. But if it clings to God, if it seeks to be wrapt round in the Eternal Love, the consciousness will come at last that the redeemed life is a unity, a glory, a growth, and that this is the will of God, even our sanctification.

And once more St. Paul teaches us that this

growing glory of life will soon and for ever be perfected. No matter what ruins we have left behind us, the towers of the New Jerusalem flash up in the unsearchable light. The white radiance of eternity is before us, stained no more by time. In the epistle from which our motto is taken St. Paul describes suffering in every form. But suffering is after all for the moment, and love is everlasting. We may look at the past and the future, and the worst they hold, in peace. He will swallow up these deaths in victory, be sure. We shall stand at the well-head of living waters and thirst no more. The bright thread of love holds together and illuminates all experience, and we rejoice in the unswerving hope of the glory of God.

And hope maketh not ashamed, because the love of God is shed abroad in our hearts by the Holy Ghost who is given unto us.

GIVERS AND RECEIVERS

THAT humanity may be parted easily into the two classes of givers and receivers is a fact which is written plainly on the very face of life. There is no such thing as fair exchange. The broad truth about some is that their lives have been spent in loving and imparting; the broad truth about others is that they have throughout coveted and received. Take, for example, the fortunes of love. Does it not seem as if the most royal faculty of the soul were often the most disordered and vagrant? How much love runs to waste, meets with no answer, is bestowed foolishly, madly! To the most loving the world is often loveless, and they are forced to think that they have nothing to draw with, and the well is deep. Even when there is a response, it is meagre and unsatisfying. Sydney Dobell, in his poem, "The Captain's Wife," tells suggestively the story of an affection returned and yet not returned.

> "Yet there is something here within this breast,
> Which, like a flower that never blossoms, lieth,
> And though in words and tears my sorrow crieth,
> I know that it hath never been expressed.
> Something that blindly yearneth to be known,
> And doth not burn, nor rage, nor leap, nor dart;
> But struggles in the sickness of my heart
> As a root struggles in a vault of stone."

For multitudes of men and women the chief bitterness of bereavement is the remorse for misprizing the treasure of a heart. Only when death has snapped the bond do they understand that what they miss and must miss all the days is the touch, the breath, the tread of love.

The same is true of impulse and service. The palmary instance for Christians is that of the Apostle and High Priest of our profession. It is true that Our Lord came to confront the empire of evil. He did not shrink from the shock of battle, but He came loving and seeking love. "He came not to be ministered unto, but to minister, and to give His life a ransom for many." If there had been given to Him no vision of a harvest in the far future, might He not have looked upon the travail of His soul as vain?

What was true of the Master is true of the disciples. It was true for St. Paul, it is true sooner or later for every faithful minister. No life of Christian service but is to be known by the mark of the nails. One of the most successful and beloved of modern preachers wrote: "I have much observed of late how the afternoon of life seems to lose part of its natural, well-deserved recompense. I know and have heard of a good many personal experiences of this kind both in Church and State. The real spirit and character of the persons affected are brought out by such trials." In the sphere of public life no truth impresses itself more deeply on the close observer than this. The reader of Mr. Morley's often finely felt pieces on political leaders must be familiar with the French saying, which comes in so often as a gloomy refrain: "In order to love mankind one must expect little from them." Early in life Burke warned a young man entering public life to regard and see well to the common people, whom his best instincts and his highest duties led him to love and to serve, but to put as little trust in them as in princes. The same statesman elsewhere describes an honest public life as carrying on a poor, unequal conflict against the passions and prejudices of our day, perhaps with no better weapons than passions and prejudices of our own. How rarely does a great leader witness the final triumph of the cause to which he has given his life! Even if many years are granted him, and he attains the glory of a feeble victory, in the height of the sunshine the shadow is rapidly stealing on. The scene often undergoes a strange transformation, final for this life. By the time the splendid career is closed, men have forgotten it in the worship of other luminaries.

There is something difficult and strange about all this. It would be far more difficult if it were not that, after all, the givers and not the receivers are the blessed. Our Lord, the great Giver, left His witness to this. "It is more blessed to give than to receive." Men, in spite of themselves, are compelled in their secret souls to admit that His judgment was right, only they will not act upon it. The great ambition of life for the vast majority is to receive. They give grudgingly, they accept eagerly; and they fancy that the more they possess the more joyous, peaceful, secure their life will be. Yet who does not know that to bear all things, to believe all things, to hope all things, to meet every defeat and refusal with an unfailing and Christlike sweetness, is the true path of peace? Who does not know that there is something better than possession?

> "The strength and the loving to gaze on each thing
> That they have not, with joy in its beauty, and sing,
> To some He hath given."

Upon these, as the beautiful German saying has it, the sun smiles, while it only shines upon others. They who love, and they only, live the true life of humanity. Better to be the loving mother than the unloving son. Demas forsook Paul because he loved this present world, but St. Paul, passing through the chequered scenes of a career full of triumph and of failure, missing love where he loved abundantly, and dying in poverty and solitude, was happier than Demas in Thessalonica, whatever his possessions were. Even men of the world know this to be true in every hour that holds the soul above itself.

For the givers receive the best. What is denied by their fellows is bestowed by God, or rather God has provided some better thing for them. If the horizon were closed by the world of sense and time, it might seem as if the receivers had the best of it, but the homely saying holds—"It was never yet loving that emptied the heart, nor giving that emptied the purse." Why? Because there is a miraculous divine supply, which counteracts and reverses the forces that might impoverish and drain. We cannot give, it is obvious, without first of all receiving. The givers have the richest hearts to begin with; the more they give, the richer their hearts grow, the sweeter and fuller is their life. They pass from duty to duty, from experience to experience, living heartily in them all, bearing everywhere a sweet savour of Christ, with an influence pervasive in proportion as they have grace to pass through worldly solicitations unaltered and unbeguiled.

How does Christ give to and bless His givers? Not so much by the permanent alteration of their circumstances, though He sometimes memorably blesses even in outward ways those who keep an open heart. More often, however, the circumstances remain, and Christ's gift is victory over them. The ultimate promise stands, "Verily thou shalt be fed." To this there is oftentimes no addition, because no addition is needed. It is still as it was in Our Lord's time. Those who have the royal heart are never left without the means of giving, never left unhappy. " He said unto them, When I sent you forth without purse, and scrip, and shoes, lacked ye anything? And they said, Nothing." It is a hopeful sign of reaction against the hungry materialism of the times that so many Christian people are turning their thoughts to the inner, present, spiritual blessings, that lift us above circumstance, that may be ours for the asking, that are bestowed instantly, in their beginnings at least, and that lift the soul into the royalty of inward happiness. We cannot live and be blessed as we are. There the givers and receivers agree. But for the receivers the blessing is found in the outward, for the givers the true riches are an inward possession. "Be not drunk with wine wherein is excess, but be filled with the Spirit" wherein there is no excess. The condemnation of the outward is in this, that it ever tends towards excess. The craving is increased by that which feeds it, the stimulations that thrill the heart for a moment need to be made stronger, and the reaction steadily becomes swifter and more complete. But the gift of the Spirit, which raises us above time and nature, brings enduring strength and peace, and can never be sought or bestowed in over-measure. It will be poured into the open thirsty heart, filling it with unstinted joy and love and energy, putting within our reach all the resources of God, making us rich to enrich the world. Time and circumstance, sorrow and impoverishment—over these we may be more than conquerors.

> "One eve, 'mid autumns far away,
> I walked alone beside a river; grey
> And pale was earth, the heavens were grey and pale,
> As if the dying year and dying day
> Sobbed out their lives together, wreaths of mist
> Stole down the hills to shroud them while they kissed
> Each other sadly; yet behind this veil
> Of dreariness and decay my soul did build,
> To music of its own, a temple filled
> With worshippers beloved that hither drew
> In silence; then I thirsted not to hear
> The voice of any friend, nor wished for dear
> Companion's hand firm clasped in mine; I knew,
> Had such been with me, they had been less near."

CHRIST WAITING TO BE GRACIOUS

AMONG the Logia or professed Sayings of Our Lord recently found in an early Greek papyrus, none has excited more perplexity than the fifth. It begins with a reminiscence of the great words which have been called the true charter of the Church—"Where two or three are gathered together in my name, there am I in the midst of them." It goes on, "Raise the stone, and there thou shalt find me; cleave the wood, and there am I." We do not accept the addition as a saying of Christ, but it is at the least a comment of high interest. Any satisfactory interpretation must read it in the light of what precedes it, and show it as exegetical or explanatory of that. For this reason various interpretations that have found currency are out of court. Let us try whether it is possible to weave the passages into one. Whether our interpretation is right or not, the truths which underlie it are of unending significance and worth.

We read the passage as a whole as meaning in the first place, that Christ waits to be gracious. When His people go to gather together in His name, they find that He is already there. He welcomes with a smile the first worshippers. He has prevented them with the blessings of His goodness. It is not as in the days after His resurrection when the disciples were within, and the door was shut, and Jesus came through and stood in the midst of them, and said, "Peace be unto you." Many of our readers, we are sure, count as among the highest and most luminous hours of life the little prayer-meetings they have attended in humble places, in kitchens and barns. It all comes before them so vividly that they are tempted to think that no experiences have been graven so deep as these. They recall the walk to the meeting-place, perhaps on a moonlit night of snow, the long shadows, the "holier day," the hopeful loneliness, the sense that they were on the road to Christ, to a full manifestation of His presence. Thus we come to the low doorway through which love, and grief, and patience, and hope approach Him, and enter the little room where we mark His blest abode, and into glory peep. The little company of grave, subdued worshippers gradually take their places, and one is aware of the deep still current of thought flowing towards the present Christ, the growing sense of His mastery over us, of His awful righteousness, and of His more awful love. Clouds are there, and they may be very heavy. There are sad thoughts—thoughts of the lapses of a stained life, of sorrows so black that scarcely a pale beam shines through them, of bereavements that have left life cold and dark as the later hours of a winter day. It may even be that the very faculty of emotion fails and sinks under the subduing weight of depression and care. But it is amidst these clouds that the Heavenly Star arises. We feel in a little that we have come into the presence of the personal Christ, that we are looking in His face, that we hear His voice and feel His heart beating. He has not cast away His people whom He foreknew. Gradually there rises the strong tide of "joy for pardoned guilt," gradually we pass into a deeper compliance with His will. We realise the worth of what we rebelled against in the days of our darker ignorance, and at last, as Christ is preached in a mystery, the heart leaps up from the past pain like a bird from its nest, and the brooding sadness fades from the face. Then is our mouth filled with laughter, and our tongue with singing, and long ere the meeting is done we know that new, strong cords have been twisted that link His life with ours.

But the human soul never speaks more truly than when it says, "I cannot come to Him unless He first come to me." He always comes first. "Raise the stone, and there thou shalt find me; cleave the wood, and there am I." The deeper thought of salvation ever stretches back to anchor itself in the uncaused Love. Redemption is not an afterthought, but an eternal thought. It is not we who ascend heaven to bring Christ down from above, it is He who comes and unites Himself with us. God's rich mercy is long kept, and it is from everlasting to everlasting. The Redeemer was anointed from all eternity to save the yet unborn world. "Lo, I come," was His word of quick obedience in the time before time was. The vitality of Calvinism lies in its assurance that love is not a thing that began yesterday and may end to-morrow, but that it foreknew, and fore-ordained, and will ultimately glorify. "Alpha art Thou indeed," are the words in which one of the deepest students of these mysteries closes his meditations. Christ is Alpha and Christ is Omega. He is the beginning and the end, the first and the last.

The second thought is that His people may find Christ when they seek Him in the strangest places. They may have the stone to raise; they may have to worship, and they have often worshipped, in dens and caves of the earth. In the Epistle to the Hebrews, which is at once so passionate and so calm, the writer's voice sometimes breaks, as when in his recital of the sufferings of the saints, "They wandered about in sheepskins and goatskins, being destitute, afflicted, tormented," he suddenly pauses to say, "of whom the world was not worthy." But the saints, even when they hide from an hourly expected vengeance, and know by every testimony that can impress man that their cause is lost, meet Christ in their hiding-place, and hear Him say, "Be of good cheer, I have overcome the world." An old author said, when his chief friend died, "The theatre of all my actions is fallen." This can never be said by true believers. The theatre of their actions can never fall when it is Christ, and He is never so near as when they are at the lowest ebb of fortune, and even nigh despair. "Raise the stone, and there shalt thou find me." It has been said with truth about Coleridge and the wonderful reach of his thoughts, "Go where you will, to the loneliest heights or the lowermost parts of the earth, in the regions of criticism and pure speculation, you are sure to find carved on the rocks the initials S. T. C." Christ's people find in the loneliest heights and in the lowest parts of the earth the Real Presence. Stones are to them consecrated bits of the old earth, like that stone of Shechem which was a witness to the people lest they denied their God.

"Cleave the wood, and there am I." The kingdom of heaven sometimes suffers violence and the violent take it by force. They may have forcibly to break through closed doors to find a place of security for their prayers. Even so He will be there before them. He has passed through the closed door like a spirit invisible to mortal eyes. Cleave the wood, burst open the door, make your way to me by any means or to any place, and still there am I. To quote Phillips Brooks: "In the deepest depths to which he can go, man shall still find Christ waiting, and hear Christ speak. And out of the heart of the unknown must come the Christ he knows so well, saying, 'I am here too.'"

"WOMEN RECEIVED THEIR DEAD"

THAT this life is a haunted house built on the very confines of the land of darkness and the shadow of death, that we are united by a thousand fibres with the other world, is denied by few. The author of the Epistle to the Hebrews in his undismayed way infinitely extends this truth for all who hold his faith. We are come, said he (not we shall come), to the eternal realities even now. For at this very moment true believers touch angels and perfected spirits, and are come to these even as they are come to God and to the blood of Jesus. Now amid the mists, the sins, the shakings of mortality, we are in the midst of fairer and stabler things. For we are come to Zion, exalted above the mountains, to draw, like a loadstone, all tossing hearts. We are now verily dwelling in the temple palace, which is the home of the Great King. We have our citizenship in the new Jerusalem, which is the mother of us all. In that Jerusalem, and in its mountain, we worship the Father. We need no longer utter the cry of homelessness, and envy the sparrow that hath found a house and the swallow that hath built a nest for herself, for we, else unsheltered, have reached a home for ourselves, even the altars of the Lord of Hosts.

But faith is needed for the constant peaceful realisation of our present citizenship above, and because faith often trembles, because the veil which in our best moments is rent asunder, or thinned at least, often seems to hang impenetrable over what we would fain see, God has come into our life, and deigned to give the proof of what faith assures us. For it is the same writer to the Hebrews who tells us that women received their dead raised to life again, or rather women received their dead by resurrection, and he remembers one other at least who received her dead in a better way. He recalls Eleazar, the heroic mother, and her seven sons mentioned in the second book of Maccabees, who were stretched on the wheel and beaten to death, rejecting the deliverance that was offered to them at the price of their principles, in order that they might obtain a better resurrection than any return to this mortal life. The King of the world shall raise us up, they said, unto everlasting life.

Women received their dead. The writer is thinking of the widow of Sarepta and of the Shunammite. He recalls how one, after many days when the barrel of meal wasted not, neither did the cruse of oil fail, lost her son, and felt that famine would have been better than the heavenly miracle. He recalls how the prophet stretched himself on the child, and the Lord hearkened, and the soul of the child came into him again, and he revived, and Elijah delivered him to his mother. He remembers the little lad who said to his father, "My head, my head," who was carried to his mother and sat on her knees till noon, and then died. He remembers how the child's body lay on the bed of the man of God through the slow torturing hours till his flesh waxed warm, and he opened his eyes. He remembers how Elisha called the Shunammite and said, "Take up thy son," and how ere she did, she fell at his feet and bowed herself to the ground. And can it be so? Did love verily melt the iron rim of fate that surrounds this weeping world of change? Yes, for when our

Lord, "with woman's blood in Him," appeared in the flesh, He, too, had compassion even as His prophets before Him, and delivered her son to the widow of Nain and Lazarus to his sisters. The beginning at Sarepta and Shunem was the dusky dimness just broken by these shafts of light. When Christ came the solemn day was breaking, and yet the full light was far off.

Women received their dead. The writer does not say men, although it is true that Jairus received his daughter. But what could pass the love of women? The power to live in others, which is their gracious prerogative and happiest attribute, is also their keenest agony. It is woman that suffers the most, although her feeling may be better hidden at first than man's. We may not see so obviously in her case the violence and the much bleeding that come with sorrow, but it is woman who tries to arrest the inevitable doom, who would detain the soul so swiftly passing, who counts in awful agonised moments every beat of the pendulum, who says even when long years have passed, and when a happiness comes again, "Oh, is there anything in heaven or in earth that can make amends for the despair of these hours?" Despair has been so utter, so awful, so God-compelling, that it rolled back the very gates of death.

But why are they now closed? Mothers have suffered every day pangs as terrible as tore the hearts of the woman of Shunem and the widows of Sarepta and Nain, and yet the dead remain. Was it for nothing, then, that these miracles were done? No, they give us perhaps our most enlarged measure of the everlasting tenderness. No tenderness was ever done by God, could ever be imagined by man, more grateful than this—the restoration of a child to his mother. It tells how well He keeps them, for though they had taken that far, swift journey they soon came back, the flush of health mantling in their cheeks. What God did for these mothers He would do for every mother if only it was best.

And is it best? Is it what mothers in their very hearts desire, to receive their dead again? The dead whom they have watched, "patient as a midnight lamp," on whom they have lavished inexpressible love and tenderness, would they have them back? The honours of the returning dead were dear bought, for all had to come again —the pain, the sickness, the sorrow, the death.

They died twice, and it is more merciful that we should die once. One can hardly believe that these restored children erred from the path, but doubtless they sinned and suffered like others. Do we not say as our eyes grow clearer, How excellent are the redeemed! how blessed are the unblemished children of life! how fair are they in the " moonlight of eternal peace, solemn and very sweet!" A greater hope, even the hope of a better resurrection, enters strangely through the rents and fissures of the broken heart, till mothers are able to say quietly, even thankfully, " I shall go to him, but he shall not return to me."

We pass from this little ring of victorious mothers to the great company of those who have had to make peace with death. Women received their dead. Do we remember that women in heaven are always receiving their dead? They are expecting them, and they are welcoming them. The happiness of the blessed is buoyant and elastic, not passionless, dreamless, changeless. There is a Sabbath-keeping for the people of God, but the Sabbath is a high day and a holiday. The mind does not eddy quietly round and round itself instead of sweeping onward. The blessedness is being evermore broken and heightened by fresh joys and hopes, and surely the sweetest of all is the entrance of redeemed souls. We have all felt when some died that it was only as it should be, that they were more needed in the other world even than they could be in this, that some heart had a greater claim upon them, and could not be content without them, and it has seemed as if their welcome must not be delayed any longer, and as if it were left to us simply for the future to make sure that we are come to the innumerable company of angels, and the spirits of the just made perfect. The joys of the angels we know are made more poignant and keen by the repentance of souls. The joys of the blessed dead are immeasurably heightened by the receiving of their own. Nothing can seem more solitary than the passage into the other life, and yet it is not solitary. " I will come again and receive you unto myself, that where I am ye may be also." That is company, and other company is waiting. There are "the shining, shining hosts of saints, the angels' burning tiers," but there are more than these.

Where the child shall greet the mother,
And the mother greet the child;

> Where dear families are gathered,
> That were scattered on the wild.

And so in the full sense heaven is home.

And at the end, whereof the dawn of Easter prophesies, women will receive their dead in another fashion, and completely, everlastingly. The day will break jubilant, as if sorrow, sighing, and death were a dream of the night. Tears, and groans, and wailings, and sobs, and broken hearts will be done away for ever as the scattered tribes of God ascend His Holy Hill. It has been well with the dead. They have been absent from the body, but present with their Lord, as if Christ robed and homed them. Yet they have waited for the adoption, to wit, the redemption of the body, and at last it has fully come. They behold one another as they once did here, and there is to be no more separation. The reunion of that day of days, its resurrection, is better than any resurrection to earth, than any brief reunion in this world. We have longed to receive our dead, to roll the great stone away, to carry captivity captive, to hear again the words that of old bowed our hearts. We have imagined that a future in this world with the dead restored would be a future from which all sorrow was expelled. But it could not be. The mother will say when she receives the little one that has been so long in the more immediate keeping of Christ that it has been well with the child. The son who has desired the mother, and prayed for her return, will rejoice that her rest has been unstirred.

> Oh rise, and sit in soft attire!
> Wait but to know my soul's desire!
> I'd call thee back to earthly days,
> To cheer thee in a thousand ways!
> Ask but this heart for monument,
> And mine shall be a large content!
>
> A crown of brightest stars to thee!
> How did thy spirit wait for me,
> And nurse thy waning light, in faith
> That I would stand 'twixt thee and death
> Then tarry on thy bowing shore,
> Till I have asked thy sorrows o'er!
>
> Because that I of thee was part,
> Made of the blood-drops of thy heart;
> My birth I from my body drew,
> And I upon thy bosom grew;
> My life was set thy life upon;
> And I was thine, and not my own.
>
> Because I know there is not one
> To think of me as thou hast done,
> From morn till starlight year by year;
> For me thy smile repaid thy tear;
> And fears for me, and no reproof,
> When once I dared to stand aloof!

> My punishment, that I was far
> When God unloosed thy weary star!
> My name was in thy faintest breath,
> And I was in thy dream of death;
> And well I know what raised thy head,
> When came the mourner's muffled tread!

It is better to rest in the Day of Redemption, and to rejoice in that Spirit whereby we are sealed unto it with joy unspeakable and full of glory. The Good Shepherd when He spoke of the sheep for whom He laid down His life, and for whom He took it again, says, "I know my sheep, and am known of mine." And in Him the long-lost communion is renewed and the long-sought good is found. In the resurrection morning each of His people says, "I have found Him whom my soul loveth—Him and them."

THE THEOLOGY OF LITTLE CHILDREN

FROM various quarters we hear at present that little children need no theology. Mr. Birrell, in a recent speech, went as far as to say that they could not be taught theology, and that whatever the priests might do, the little ones were deaf to their teaching. Mr. Birrell is a minister's son, and to such as he occasional sallies into the field of dogma are necessary, no matter what they have kept or lost of their first faith. Professor Bruce, who is held in deserved respect as a thoroughly trained theologian, and one whose conclusions are in the main those of the catholic Church, has compiled a religious catechism for children published as a sequel to his book, "With Open Face." In this he asks and answers questions about the earthly life of Jesus. He recognises that Christ performed miracles of healing. He tells the children that they should love Christ with all their hearts as their Saviour, and worship and serve Him as their Lord. But about the Resurrection he has nothing to say, and about the present activity of Jesus there is only one question and answer—"Where is Jesus now?—He is in the house of his Father in heaven, where He is preparing a place for all who bear His name and walk in His footsteps." There the catechism ends. A book of religion for children, which has been widely circulated and much praised by orthodox divines, slurs over in a few sentences the Resurrection, the Ascension, and the eternal reign. And there is a section of Nonconformists at present who think the problem of religious education in public schools might be solved by confining the instruction to the earthly life of Jesus. It is obvious to remark that they would be confronted at once with the question of miracle. But our purpose at present is rather to show that little children are from the first taught a theology which is deep and catholic, taught it by their earliest instructors, and taught it in those hymns whereby God stills the enemy and the avenger.

Our appeal is to the hymnals which have been provided in all sections of the Church for the use of children. For convenience sake we shall use that of the late Dr. W. Fleming Stevenson, who was a man of great catholicity and fine literary taste.

It will be admitted by all who are familiar with the movements of theology during the last fifty years that the deeper current has been running and is running more strongly than ever towards faith in the great revealing acts of God. There is a Broad Churchism which has run to seed, which is practically dead in the Establishment, and which is dying everywhere in Dissent. There is another Broad Churchism which is broad in the sense that it has insisted on the hallowing of all life by the Incarnation, and that is living and growing. When "Essays and Reviews" appeared, many blundering people could see no difference between their teaching and that of Maurice and his immediate disciples. Maurice passionately protested against the association. He refused to accept the name of Broad Churchman. We can see now that he was right. He was not content with believing vaguely in an inward spiritual relation; he knew that there must be a saving faith in the divine acts by which the divine light has an external as well as an internal manifestation. It is by these acts, by the Incarnation, the Atonement, and the Resurrection of our Lord that we get our one true glimpse of eternal Being. Now we take our children's hymnal, and everywhere we find these great acts affirmed and interpreted. The earthly life of Jesus is everywhere remembered as it should be, but the eternal life of the Father and the Son which existed before man and exists now, is held to give these words and works all their meaning. Without this present life of Jesus, the past life would mean very little. It would be indeed a heroic and pathetic memory, but it could not reinforce us in our need, and when it was considered attentively, it might seem as if they had much to say for themselves who regarded it as a shattered dream, a broken song, a magnificent failure. But everywhere the hymns teach the holy Incarnation. Did Jesus gather the children about Him in Palestine, and bless them, and lay His hands on their hair? He can do the same to-day.

> " Thou who here didst prove
> To babes so full of love,
> Thou art the same above,
> Merciful Jesus."

Did He once still the raging waters of the lake?

> "O well we know it was the Lord,
>   Our Saviour and our Friend;
> Whose care of those who trust His Word
>   Will never, never end."

Do children wish now to have been with Christ in the days of His flesh when He called the little ones as lambs to His fold? They will be with Him yet, and not only may they have the same blessing now, but they will have it to the very fullest hereafter.

> "In the beautiful place He has gone to prepare
>   For all that are washed and forgiven;
> And many dear children are gathering there,
>   For of such is the kingdom of heaven."

Was He born a babe in the manger? His birth was proclaimed by the angels.

> "For they knew that the child on Bethlehem's Hill
>   Was Christ the Lord."

Did He come to Sion bringing His salvation to the children who praised His name?

> "Since the Lord retaineth
>   His love for children still,
> Though now as King He reigneth
>   On Sion's heavenly hill,
> We'll flock around His banner
>   Who sits upon the throne,
> And cry the loud Hosannah
>   To David's royal Son."

Are children taught to sing the mystery of His great oblation? Do they understand the Cross as the final manifestation of divine love and of human need?

> "Glory be to Jesus,
> Who, in bitter pains,
> Poured for me the life blood
> From His sacred veins.
>
> Abel's blood for vengeance
> Pleaded to the skies;
> But the blood of Jesus
> For our pardon cries."

Can children be taught that He was born to die, that He came to save them by dying, and that now He pleads for them a Priest for ever?

> "Oh what has Jesus done for me?
> He pitied me, my Saviour;
> My sins were great, His love was free,
> He died for me, my Saviour.
> Exalted by the Father's side,
> He pleads for me, my Saviour;
> A heavenly mansion He'll provide
> For all who love the Saviour."

Above all, if we may say so, these hymns are saturated with the thought of the Resurrection and the eternal reign. He was the King of Glory ere He came to seek us. He is the King of Glory now that He has returned from the wilderness. It is hardly worth while to show the pitiful mutilations and omissions to which the Unitarians in their hymnal for children are compelled to resort. In Reginald Heber's "By cool Siloam's shady rill," the closing verses are:

> "O Thou whose infant feet were found
>   Within Thy Father's shrine,
> Whose years, with changeless virtue crowned,
>   Were all alike divine;
>
> Dependent on Thy bounteous breath,
>   We seek Thy grace alone,
> In childhood, manhood, age, and death,
>   To keep us still thine own!"

In the Unitarian hymnal the lines read:

> "O thou whose infant feet were led
>   Within thy Father's shrine,
> Whose years, with holiest spirit fed,
>   Were all alike divine;
>
> We seek that spirit's bounteous breath,
>   We ask his grace alone,
> In childhood, manhood, age, and death,
>   To keep us still thine own."

When the young gather to dedicate themselves to God it seems as if they could not but lift up their eyes to the Light, the Way, the Truth, the Life.

> "O Light, O Way, O Truth, O Life,
>   O Jesu, born mankind to save,
> Give Thou Thy peace in deadliest strife,
>   Shed Thou Thy calm on stormiest wave ;
> Be Thou our Hope, our Joy, our Dread,
> Lord of the living and the dead."

More than that, one of the most noble of children's hymns dares to touch on the subduing mystery of a child's death, and its far journey to the new home :

> " Little travellers Zionward,
>   Each one entering into rest,
> In the Kingdom of your Lord,
>   In the mansions of the blest ;
> There, to welcome, Jesus waits,
>   Gives the crowns His followers win.
> Lift your heads, ye golden gates,
>   Let the little travellers in."

Now these great Acts of God when applied in their practical bearing simply mean that Christ is close to the very fountains of the human spirit, that we can pray to Him, and that we ought to pray to Him. The Ritschlian teaching passionately denies this. We have no contact with Christ, it affirms, save through such facts as remain to us of His early life. But then this school denies His incarnation, denies His atonement, denies His resurrection, and denies His heavenly reign. We are always baffled to understand how orthodox theologians can discuss their differences with the Ritschlians as if they were talking of nothing more important than the conformation of a beetle. It is no wonder that such men should revive the view that Christ is a moralist speaking with authority, giving an example, and wielding in some way the power of judgment and punishment. They view the Church as "a virtue-making institution," making virtue by teaching what Christ did and said in Palestine. The Church is indeed a virtue-making institution, but she makes virtue by directing her children to the accessible and ever-flowing spiritual spring and source of virtue. The Church teaches the vital and organic relation of all believing hearts with Jesus Christ Himself. She teaches that into the secret recesses of the believing heart Christ pours the Divine Spirit, that believers are continually fed as the apostles were fed by Christ their Life, by Christ within them, by Christ the Inspirer and Enabler of all good. Now that means that Christ is to be addressed in prayer, for if He speaks to the spirit of man directly, surely the spirit of man may and must speak in return to Him. If our life and peace are consciously drawn from Christ, we must bless Him for what He has given and plead with Him to give us more. To pray to Christ as if He were more merciful than the Father is indeed condemned from every fact of the divine revelation. But even as we pray to the Father, so we may pray to the Eternal Son. We can hold communion as direct with any one Person of the Blessed Trinity as with another. Now the peculiarity of children's hymns is that they are almost all prayers to the Lord Jesus.

> "Jesus, tender Shepherd, hear me;
> Bless Thy little lamb to-night."

Is that prayer answered? Is it true that the Great Shepherd is beside His lambs when they sleep and when they wake?

> "Yet still to His footstool in prayer I may go,
> And ask for a share of His love."

Is that a faithful saying, and worthy of all acceptation?

> "Holy Jesus, every day
> Keep us in the narrow way."

Does He then guide the feet of His children home? We ask for no theology beyond what we find in the hymns sung by little children, sung with the understanding as well as with the voice. The mysteries of God are spoken there so far as human lips may speak them. When it pleased God to reveal His Son in Paul, He was revealed not only as the Lord of Glory, but as the very life of his life. So the Apostle said: "Though we have known Christ after the flesh, yet now henceforth know we Him so no more." It was not that St. Paul disparaged the historical life of Jesus. Every word and every deed kept for us is precious beyond price. But the meaning would pass from them; they would become bleached, and faded, and outworn if we did not know that they are perpetual signs of an activity that is constant, of a love and care that never cease, so that they are all transfigured by the glory that excelleth. Let every mother who reads these words ask what religion would be to her if she were told that she must no more teach her children to pray to Jesus, that she must no more teach them that He is the King of heaven, that she cannot speak to them of His present life, but only of His past, that He will not be with them in the long journey they can never take with her.

THE EVANGELICAL LOVE FOR CHRIST

IN his admirable portrait of Coventry Patmore, published in the *Contemporary Review*, Mr. Gosse tells us that Patmore prepared a book entitled "Sponsa Dei." It was a mystical interpretation of the love between the soul and God by an analogy of the love between a woman and a man—in fact, a transcendental treatise on divine desire seen through the veil of human desire. Mr. Gosse assures us that the purity and crystalline passion of the writer carried him safely over the most astounding difficulties. But Mr. Patmore decided to burn it. Perhaps it was better so. His theme, however, has engaged many Christian hearts, and it has been especially expounded in mystical interpretations of the Song of Songs. We have before us a volume entitled "The Most Holy Place: Sermons on the Song of Solomon," by

Mr. Spurgeon.* Whatever ground there be for the spiritual interpretation of Canticles—and scholars generally reject it—there is no doubt that we have in this volume a most valuable contribution to Christian literature. The Church does not yet know what a great saint and doctor she possessed in Mr. Spurgeon. If religion is to be derived from revelation, and if theology is to be kept close to Christian experience, living or dying therewith, then we do not hesitate to say that Mr. Spurgeon was not a whit behind the very chiefest of theologians. Of course, what little criticism there is in the book is of small account, and it does not profess to be important. What is important is the depth of Christian knowledge the book discloses, and we have no hesitation in saying that it is one of the greatest treatises on the love of Christ to His people and on His people's love to Christ that the Church possesses, wonderful alike for fertility and exquisite delicacy of thought. The writer plays with the images of the Canticles, but always with a careful reverence and reserve. "I am the rose of Sharon and the lily of the valley," he comments upon thus: "Red as the rose in His sacrifice, white as the lily as

* Passmore and Alabaster.

He ascends on high in His perfect righteousness, clothed in His white robe of victory to receive gifts for men," and the volume is full of such beautiful fancies, though what is at the heart of it is not fancy, but the very truth of truths. Mr. Spurgeon was remarkable beyond most preachers for the passion and intensity of his personal love for Christ, and here it appears in every sentence. He was not like Dr. Newman, whose Christian creed perhaps did not vary much from the beginning to the end, and was always held with vehement conviction, but who was ever solicitous to construct defences round it, building up a new fort for every old fort that was thrown down. With apologetics Mr. Spurgeon had no concern at all. "Whereas I was blind, now I see," was the first and the last of his defences of the faith.

What is the evangelical love for Christ? What are its perennial sources and characteristics? It is not enough to say that evangelical love is an admiration for Christ. Those who do not admire Christ in a sense have sinned the sin against the Holy Ghost. Though the terrible alternative, either God or not good, logically holds, those who do not believe that

Christ was God see much in His life and teaching worthy of praise. Literary unbelief has shrunk from many words about Jesus, but when we get at the meaning of the unbelief of such men as Burns and Carlyle, we find that they thought of Christ as an amiable dreamer. It is pathetic to see how Renan endeavours to save His character. He thinks that Christ partly deteriorated as He went on vindicating His Messianic claims, and that it would have been better if He had died after preaching the Sermon on the Mount or by the well of Samaria. But he pleads that sincerity in the modern sense is not a Semitic virtue, and that all Christ's fault was that He took humanity with its illusions and sought to act upon it and with it. It is needless to say that the evangelical love of Christ rests on an implicit faith in His sinlessness. But it is more than this faith. It is more than honour, it is more than trust, it is more than obedience, it is something warmer and tenderer than all these, for it is love.

The evangelical love for Christ rests first upon His love for us. There is a love for the dead we have never known, a true love, a love that may grow with the years. Companionship with the words of a noble spirit like St. Paul may quicken the ardour of a true affection. But then there is no answering love in return. They do not love us, and have never loved us. They do not even know us, but Our Saviour knows us, has known us from the beginning—has loved us from the beginning. "Who loved *me?*" There is nothing in life which is at once so humbling and so ennobling as it is to be loved by a nature far higher and purer than our own, and, thanks be to God, it is a common experience. In every form love is precious. The love of the weak, the love of the ignorant, the love of the sinful, if it is true, is not to be lightly thought of. But it is the love of the higher bestowed upon the lower that rallies the sinking forces of life and helps us to play the man. Down into the depths and failures of our history this love comes streaming, however we may be despised of men. "Thou hast been precious in *my* sight, and honourable, and I have loved thee." There is a saying of an old mystic that it is impossible for love not to be returned in some measure or another. That may be an exaggeration, though it has its element of truth, and yet it is hard to think that any one can believe in the love of Christ to *him*, and not be constrained in some way to give the love back.

The deep foundation and the certain assurance of the love of Christ is that He died to redeem us. Whenever the heart is most kindled, it is by the thought of the well of God dug by the soldiers' spears, of the cross, the sponge, the vinegar, the nails, of the red wine of love that flowed when He trod the winepress alone, and of the people there was none with Him, of the sweet and dreadful cry, "Eli, Eli, lama sabachthani?" Perhaps every intense, passionate, human love has its foundation in some act, some sacrifice, some day of days to which the heart keeps turning in its darkness, and Mr. Spurgeon says, "I should not like to guess how heavy a true heart may sometimes become." The old hymns are full of this.

> "Love so vast that nought can bound,
> Love too deep for thought to sound;
> Love that made the Lord of all
> Drink the wormwood and the gall;
> Love which led Him to the cross,
> Bearing there unuttered loss.
>
> Love which brought Him to the gloom
> Of the cold and darksome tomb;
> Love which will not let Him rest
> Till His chosen all are blest,

> Till they all for whom He died,
> Live rejoicing by His side."

Our love flames up as we recognise that He has not in vain suffered life and death for us, that the strings that bound our burden to us begin to crack, and our load falls into His sepulchre to be seen no more. Perhaps it is true that in this love there is an element of remorse, and is not that the most quickening element in a great human affection? Few can say that they have answered back the love that was given them as they should have answered it, and at the memory every energy of the heart awakes.

> "I seem to hear your laugh, your talk, your song,
> It is not true that Love will do no wrong,
> Poor child!
> And did you think, when you so cried and smiled,
> How I, in lonely nights, should lie awake,
> And of these words your full avengers make?
> Poor child, poor child.
> And now, unless it be,
> That sweet amends thrice told are come to thee,
> O God, have Thou *no* mercy upon me,
> Poor child!"

Is not that the meaning of the Song in heaven? "Worthy is the Lamb *that was slain* to receive power, and riches, and wisdom, and strength, and honour, and glory, and blessing." He was slain, and we slew Him. We can never make it up. The thorns of the thorn-crowned head pierce the heart, the fever of His death wakes the fever of our passion till all the loves that once strayed abroad gather to a burning centre, and the fountain of our affections has but one channel, and that is He.

The evangelical love for Christ rests on the constant consciousness of His presence. He is really present. We speak to Him, we tell Him of all our weaknesses, our want, our sin, our failure, our longing. It is this which the mystics most desire to teach. Love must be able to come near, to enter into the closest, most endearing intimacies. There is a real peril in trying to parallel the sacred mysteries of the spiritual life from earthly analogies; and yet what could be more significant of the waning of Christianity than that Christians should actually be gravely discussing whether people who deny any present communion with Christ at all may not be as good Christians as those whose life-habit it is? Let us not deceive ourselves. There is no Christianity which does not mean this, and we find in the New Testament language strained and pressed to its utmost meaning in order to express this truth.

"We will come unto him, and make our abode with him," said the Son. "I live, yet not I, but Christ liveth in me," said the Apostle. The mystery of union with Christ is the ultimate mystery and experience of the Christian faith. There was one of whom it was said that he often fell asleep talking to Christ, was often heard in his dreams speaking to his Saviour, and there are multitudes now who are not speaking emptily when they say that their Redeemer has been with them this many a year.

This love of the soul for Christ is a love that trusts His love as constant and almighty. It is constant, and human love is much of it inconstant. Even where it is truest the communion may be snapped at any moment by death. And human love is weak, and cannot even by the last sacrifice accomplish what it yearns for. "Would God I had died for thee, O Absalom, my son, my son!" There is little here that we can count on. Friends fail us, death takes our truest, and yet we can count on that love which is constant in all worlds, through all years, that love in which the dead are living and the lost are found, that love which does not die when we die, that does not cease to care when we can care no longer, that love in which we and our beloved dwell as in a fortress-home. Aubrey de Vere writes of one who imagines herself dead and her lover living alone, and then, reproaching herself, remembers the love which can still be his:

> " Upon my gladness fell a gloom;
> Thee saw I—on some far-off day—
> My Husband, by thy loved one's tomb;
> I could not help thee where I lay.
>
> Ah, traitress I, to die the first!
> Ah, hapless thou to mourn alone!
> Sudden that truth upon me burst,
> Confessed so oft, till then unknown—
>
> There *lives* who loved him! loves and loved
> Better a million-fold than I!
> That love with countenance unremoved
> Looked on him from eternity.
>
> That love of wisdom and of power,
> Though I were dust would guard him still,
> And faithful at the last dread hour,
> Stand near him whispering, ' Fear no ill.' "

This evangelical love for Christ is then a passionate love. There is on earth the vividness of first love, the fervour of early passion, and this finds its likeness in the Christian's love for Christ. But there is on earth a love nobler than that, a love that glows with a great, steady ardour, with a still, intense, vehement flame, and this is the Christian ideal. This is the love that labours when all labour without it would be hard and heavy. This is the love that fights when all seems dead against it. This is the love that lifts up its spear against ten thousand, and turns the strength of the foemen at the gates. This is the love that welcomes suffering for the beloved's sake. Sacrifice is continually changing its form, but it is always present in the life of the Christian. Where it is most present there is love warmest and kindest. When Ignatius was led to his martyrdom, and thought of the nearness of his death and pain, he said, "Now I begin to be a Christian." Well has it been said that wherever the Church goes the thick smoke of her suffering ascends to heaven. "We are alway delivered to death for Jesus' sake."

THE THEOLOGY OF WALTER PATER*

THE alienation between literature and the Church is at last recognised as a serious and formidable fact. And the idea has gained currency that if large parts of the Christian dogma could be abandoned or thrown into the shade, the result would be a religion acceptable to the cultured. If it were so, our duty would in no wise be changed. We should still have to declare *all* the counsel of God. We should still have to say, " I have received of the Lord that which I deliver unto you." Otherwise preaching descends to the level of speech-making. But we maintain that it is not so, that a volatilised Christianity has no more attraction for the man of letters than it has for the rest of mankind. A very striking proof of this may be

---

* Essays in the *Guardian*. By Walter Pater. Privately printed.

found in a curious little volume of which one hundred copies only have been printed for private circulation. This contains nine reviews contributed to the *Guardian* by Mr. Walter Pater. Mr. Gosse, we believe, has edited the volume, and that distinguished critic correctly says that though the positive value of the essays may be slight, they are of value and interest as proceeding from Mr. Pater. It seems to us that they are of very eminent value in helping us to understand the exact theological position in which he finally rested. It is quite superfluous to say that Pater was an ideal exponent of the culture of his day.

In "Marius the Epicurean," his most elaborate and living book, Mr. Pater enforces and enlarges the philosophy of his work on the Renaissance. It is expressed in few words: A counted number of pulses is given us of varied dramatic life. We have an interval, and then our place knows us no more. Our business is to expend that interval in getting as many pulsations as possible into the given time. This might be called Epicureanism; the author calls it New Cyrenaeicism. When the glamour of youth dies away, something more is needed than this philosophy of moments. Life seeks pathetically for continuity, for what lasts and binds, and can be handed on from soul to soul. That continuity it finds in the ancient and wonderful ethical order which is in impregnable possession of humanity. The crystallised feeling that is stored in the world's moral belief attracts the seeker for pleasure. Pleasure is not to be found as he first thought, in the violation of this moral order, but in submission to it. His sceptical attitude may be, and indeed is, still maintained. Morality may have no absolute virtue or validity, but obedience is a source of pleasure and quickening faculty to the individual. It will be seen that we have advanced to morality, but not beyond Epicureanism. A further step is taken towards religion, and it is in the same direction. Christianity may not be true, but it is best to treat it as if it were. True Christian feeling gives brightness and sweetness to life and mitigates the awfulness of death. Christianity enshrines much of the most heroic and noble feeling and utterance of the human spirit. Therefore it is wise to take it on trust. The intellectual citadel should be kept inviolate. You may think, if you please, with the elect who are the small minority. But you will be wise to give yourself at the same time to the prayers and tears and dreams of the the majority. In this way the sweetest, most elusive, most delicate flavour will be given to life and death will lose something of its terror. Marius, who in reality died but a half Christian death, was generously recognised as a martyr in times when martyrdom was taken as a kind of sacrament with plenary grace.

In his unfinished last book, "Gaston de Latour," Pater goes further. His editor, Mr. Shadwell, says that the book was to be a picture of a refined and cultivated mind, capable of keen enjoyment in the pleasures of the senses and the intellect, but destined to find its complete satisfaction in that which transcends both. The final expression of Pater's mind in this book has been well summed up in the text, "I have seen that all things come to an end, but Thy commandment is exceeding broad." The utmost limits of the new ways are reached, and the restless and immortal spirit pursues its quest further and finds its large room in the commandment. It was stated, though not very prominently, when Pater died, that he had been for years a professed believer in Christ, and we owe much gratitude to Mr. Gosse for giving us the proof of this, and for indicating the lines on which Pater advanced beyond his Epicureanism. The most interesting passage is perhaps that in which he deals very courteously with Robert Elsmere. "We have little patience," says Pater, "with the liberal clergy who dwell on nothing else than the difficulties of faith and the propriety of concession to the opposite forces." He goes on to say: "As against the purely negative action of the scientific Ward, the high-pitched Gray, and the theistic Elsmere, the ritualistic priest, and the quaint Methodist, Fleming, both so admirably sketched, present perhaps no unconquerable differences. The question of the day is not between one and another of these, but in another sort of opposition, well defined by Mrs. Ward herself, between 'two estimates of life, the estimate which is the offspring of the scientific spirit, and which is for ever making the visible world fairer and more desirable in mortal eyes, and the estimate of St. Augustine.' To us," Pater goes on, "the belief in God, in goodness at all, in the story of Bethlehem, does not rest on evidence so diverse in character and force as Mrs. Ward supposes. At his death, Elsmere has started what to us would be a most unattractive place of worship, where he preaches an admirable sermon on the purely human aspect of the life of Christ. But we think there would be very few such sermons in the new church or chapel, for the interest of that life could hardly be very varied when all such sayings as 'Though He was rich, yet for our sakes He became poor,' have ceased to be applicable to it. It is the infinite nature of Christ which has led to such diversities of genius in preaching as St. Francis, and Taylor, and Wesley." Again, in his essay on Amiel he criticises Amiel's religion, and says that his profoundly religious spirit might have developed " had he been able to see that the old-fashioned Christianity is itself but the proper historic development of the true 'essence' of the New Testament. Assenting on probable evidence to so many judgments of the religious sense, he failed to see the equally probable evidence that there is for the beliefs; the peculiar direction of men's hopes, which complete those judgments harmoniously, and bring them into connection with the facts; the venerable institutions of the past, with the lives of the saints. By failure, as we think, of that historic sense of which he could speak so well, he got no further in that direction than the glacial condition of rationalistic Geneva." It is that very Genevan rationalism which is ever and anon being recommended as the specific for our ills, but Pater saw that if any powerful part of Christianity is accepted, it involves the rest, and that ultimately the witness of all the saints, and not only the experience of the individual, is to be relied upon, for it was to the saints that the faith was first of all delivered.

We go back on another typical figure of the world of culture, one who never, like Pater, completely surrendered his unbelief. Clough, whose inexplicable attraction, notwithstanding the small amount of his enduring product, continues, left a fragment belonging to the last period of his life, on "The Religious Tradition." Most readers know something of his hard battle with moral and intellectual perplexities, from the time when he went to Oxford, and was for two years, in his own words, like a straw drawn by the draught of a chimney, on to his premature death. But his later years, if they were not filled with the strange, unearthly peace which is the final token of Christ's indwelling, were much more quiet than the earlier. He had begun to see that it was not his business to construct a religion or a theology, or to achieve his own salvation. He began to recognise, though dimly, that these things were the work of Another. In his last writings he laid emphasis on the significance and depth of the moral and religious teaching which passed by the name of Christianity, and wrote that "implicit reliance cannot be placed on the individual experience, reason, judging power." Therefore, he says, "I see not what alternative any sane or humble-minded man can have but to throw himself upon the great religious tradition." His opinion on a pared-down, accommodated Christianity is seen in the words: "I contend that the Unitarian is morally and religiously only half educated compared with the Episcopalian." So it comes at last that the wisest begin to doubt themselves, begin to see how little way their individual faculties carry them, discover that Christianity is not a new thing, but that for all these centuries the Spirit has interpreted the Word to the hearts of believers. They accept some word of God-guided men, prove it in their own experience, and then, even if their experience tarries behind, they trust the inspired leader and go on with him. They have lost the desire to construct a new path to heaven; they are content to take the way which the saints have trodden, the way that leads to the Fountain.

Something may be said also of Balzac—a writer who is at last coming to his own in England. It is quite true that Balzac's novels are not for everybody, and that many of them, perhaps most, should be kept out of the hands of the young. He was the greatest of those who have explored the subterranean ways of life and set in a terrible lustre the secret things of darkness. His books are full of the tremendous pursuit of retribution, of the slowly gathering coils of fate, of the mysteries of pain and shame lying under the thin surface of life. His characters are haunted by thoughts of the past, by hopeless hopes, by devouring recollections, and he shows us—and this perhaps is his greatest achievement—that these things are to be found no less in the quiet woods and fields than in the crowded city. We will steadily refuse to say that this literature, when done grandly, has not its place and use. It brings home, as few things do, the sense of human sinfulness and human misery, and in many passages of Holy Scripture the same method is used to produce the same result. Indeed, we believe that if the Christian Church is to recover its old power, it will be in recoiling from the shallow optimism which refuses to put aside the silken curtains and see what is behind. The question of Balzac's greatness as an artist is one of criticism, and we should think few competent judges will deny that he is incomparably the finest of French novelists, and indeed the first novelist, with one exception, of the whole century. Nor must it be forgotten that he himself, notwithstanding his long, pitiful struggle, was one of the friendliest, gentlest, and kindest of men. Few records are more touching and noble than the collection of his letters, and we have dwelt again and again, with deep emotion, on many passages—on his filial love, on his invincible courage, on his impatience of the materialistic creed, on the heroism with which in his rainy garret he went on year after year without encouragement, doing his very best. And above all, where shall we find such a story of pure, tender, delicate devotion as that of his fifteen years' love, or a more pathetic episode than his death, after but three months of the long-waited happiness? That Balzac was free from follies it would be ridiculous to deny, but how much of passionate affection and devotion lay behind them! When in the end of the day death set the doors open and let the sun shine in, the closet of this man, who had drawn such pictures of the skeleton in every closet, was found empty. We have not space to make quotations, but where in the literature of fiction can one find so complete an exposition of remorse and expiation as that, for example, in his book, "The Country Pastor"? His great intellect and noble heart rested devoutly on the experience of the saints. He found no difficulty in the humble acceptance of the Christian creed, and one can imagine what scorn would have awakened in him by the gaunt and forlorn structure which is dressed out and set forth among us anew as the Christian faith. How often, even in his least ungenial writing, when he seems abandoned to the spirit of cynicism, does his faith flash up and drive it out of sight! There be those who, with Matthew Arnold, still hear the melancholy, long withdrawing roar of the sea of faith as it steadily retreats and leaves the barren shingles naked. Others, more wise, hear the wave of joy and hope that is to lift the world coming nearer and nearer.

IS THE SERMON ON THE MOUNT THE CHRISTIAN GOSPEL?*

THERE is great room for some independent and robust works of native manufacture dealing with Christian ethics. We have been too much dependent upon foreigners for instruction of this kind, and at the moment of writing the only epoch-making English contribution that we recall to this subject is the admirable work of Dr. Wace on Christianity and Morality. Mr. Strong's book is therefore very welcome. He is already known to a small circle of readers as the author of a handbook of Christian theology, which somehow strangely failed to make an impression, but which, although it has its shortcomings, contains much that is both masculine and devout. It is perhaps impossible to rate his

---

* "Christian Ethics." The Bampton Lectures for 1895. By T. B. Strong, M.A., Student of Christchurch. Longmans.

Bampton Lectures as highly, yet they will take a good place in the series, and they deserve an attentive perusal. The book is well written, although there is a lack of ring and concentration, and an amount of repetition possibly to be excused in the pulpit, but inevitably resented by the reader. All parts of the book are not of the same value. The concluding chapter on Ethics and the Church is unsatisfactory, and the same may be said of all the passages where the Church is introduced. Mr. Strong's reading, extensive and careful in some directions, is limited in others. For example, he makes no reference to Rothe and Martensen, though both, and especially the former, could have taught him very much. It is nothing short of a scandal that the great work of Rothe in Holtzmann's edition has not been translated into English. The third section of the book, the *Pflichtenlehre*, in particular, is worth all the English books on Christian ethics put together. Mr. Strong, though he has studied the Fathers and given us some fresh and interesting details of their ethical theories, is weak in the Reformation literature, and his section on the Reformation is very defective, not from any will to misrepresent, but from want of knowledge.

There is, however, much that is valuable in this book, and we propose to reproduce Mr. Strong's argument against the view that has been revived in our day, that the whole of Christianity lies in the Sermon on the Mount—in other words, that the Sermon on the Mount is the Christian Gospel. It is against this theory that he directs the whole force of his reasoning, and with complete success so far as he goes, though, as we shall see, he has almost wholly neglected a line of argument equally weighty and important with that to which he has done such justice.

Mr. Strong shows that the fault of Greek and Jewish ethics was that they commanded from without. Righteousness, therefore, could not come of them. The Jews, it is true, under the guidance of revelation, found a purer morality than the Greeks; they went deeper into the causes of moral failure, and found them in the will. All the same, that law in which they delighted could not save them, and the worship of the law produced in Judaism the most unlovely, hard, and unspiritual of all characters. For a greater depth of tenderness one had to look for those who in a sense dispensed with the law, waiting for some better thing to come, even the consolation of Israel.

When our Lord appeared and preached the Sermon on the Mount, the situation was not altered in essence. The Sermon on the Mount asserted the authority of a new teacher, and it laid stress on the spiritual virtues—in this following the loftier strain of Hebrew thought. It gave a promise of perfection—the perfection of the Father in heaven. Nevertheless it remained a law. It gave commands to the will, set before the will an ideal, but it did not give any direct promise of guidance, and it did not say how perfection was to be reached. And therefore it is true that the Sermon on the Mount kills as relentlessly as the law, nay, even more relentlessly, because it is more difficult. The heights to be scaled are impossible heights. Mr. Strong points out very frankly that whenever people have tried to obey the Sermon on the Mount from an external point of view they have failed hopelessly, and ended in utter confusion. The Sermon on the Mount constrains and presses the will at every point, closes avenues of action, and opens a path which unaided none are able to tread. So the old sober view of the Sermon on the Mount, that expressed by Dr. Robertson Smith in his words that the Sermon on the Mount was the preliminary part of Christ's work, and that its object was to show how His teaching attached itself to and transcended Jewish teaching, must stand. It is the only one that coheres with the New Testament, that coheres even with the Gospels. When we read the Gospels, we find in them very little moral exhortation, and no armoury of ethical precepts. They are largely historical anecdotes of a life, of the ideal life. St. John sees more profoundly into the springs of moral action than the Synoptics, but his book, too, is historical. It is no answer that in the case of Jesus the ideal was real, the Word was made flesh. Still the ideal remained external to the will, and such an ideal, whether expressed in the life or in the commandment, may very easily hurt rather than help. It may so confound, discourage, and abase that the impulse to moral struggle is utterly destroyed. And even as an ideal it is incomplete; no one can say that Christ has solved all, or nearly all, the problems of life. On many points He has not touched. The change of circumstances, the progress of civilisation, have called into existence many new difficulties on which, viewed from the outside, His career gives us very little light. Considered as external, this ideal, great and supreme as it is, must gradually fade away with time.

But Christ in His last hours opened His heart. He had previously been behaving very differently from the ordinary teacher of a new theory. Instead of seeking fresh disciples and larger audiences, He turned to the inner circle, and gave His force to strengthening them. He told His disciples that the Spirit of Truth would come and dwell within them, and open up the way to a complete communion between God and man. Through His death and through His rising again a new power would enter into the world. The Holy Ghost dwelling in the heart would take of the things that were Christ's, would interpret their meaning, and would give the power to fulfil them in actual experience. In other words, Christ does not so much exhort as promise. The real centre of investigation into the ethical meaning of Christianity must be transferred from the Gospel story to the time after Pentecost. Then the disciples and the world too, little though it knew it, entered into another order, in which forces had begun to stir which were able to transform sinful men into the image of the Son. Jesus was the Lord and the Mediator; His resurrection sealed His life and work with the good pleasure of God, and opened in the Holy Spirit a new spring of ethical activity which at once sharpened the perceptions of the conscience and gave power to follow them. Thus the whole notion of morality moved inward, and under all circumstances, even in the circumstances sketched in the Epistle to the Hebrews, the new faith was equal to its battle, and ready to meet whatever strain might be imposed upon it.

In this way we understand, what indeed has always been easily understood by the Christian Church, the position of the Apostles. They say very little about Christ's teaching. It is amazing how few direct references to His precepts can be discovered. But they lay the whole stress upon those points which most distinctly give evidence of the entering of the new order and the abrogation of the old, namely, the Crucifixion and the Resurrection. This fresh vital force, this bestowal of health, this power set in motion by the Holy Spirit, was to be the true deliverance of mankind—mankind that hitherto had been haunted and depressed by failure. To the Apostles the insistence on the Sermon on the Mount as the sum of Christianity would have appeared a relapse into hopeless paganism.

They felt this all the more because they understood the depths in which mankind had been plunged by the Fall. The Greeks knew nothing of a Fall, the Jews thought that the Fall might be reversed by the action of the will, but to the Apostles, as to Christ, our whole nature was touched by incapacity. The abnormal element in human nature had gained the mastery, and so we were enthralled in a captivity from which only the death and resurrection of Our Lord could set us free. Mr. Strong has some penetrating remarks on the respective tempers in which sin is treated by the Old Testament and the New. There is a passion against sin in the Old Testament, a passion all the fiercer because sin seems so strong. The New Testament treats it far more calmly. It is equally severe, perhaps more severe; it preaches the present judgment of sin as well as the day of reckoning at the Parousia, but it looks upon sin as a power that may be conquered, and that has been implicitly conquered by the death of Jesus. It finds no explanation of the life and death of Jesus that does not recognise the Fall and the Retrieval. It is little to say that the modern washed-out version of Christianity, which represents the death of Christ as a sacrifice in the sense of a resignation of good things, would have been rejected by the Apostles. It would not even have been understood by them. In that sense they did not use the word sacrifice at all.

It is the weak point of Mr. Strong's book that while he by no means rejects, but rather cordially accepts, the doctrine of the Atonement, he gives it no proper place in Christian ethics. He has one lecture, for example, on the great text of St. Paul, "We preach Christ crucified," but it is hopelessly unexegetical. He rides off on the phrase "the wisdom of God," trying to connect it with the Old Testament thought of the wisdom which was with God when He prepared the heavens. For the Apostle's word "power" he substitutes "love," and he argues that "the reason why the life of Christ has a real meaning for our lives is because in it the whole wisdom and love of God were manifested in full in their inseparable unions." He almost wholly ignores the fact that the Apostle is laying stress upon the Atonement, that his meaning is, "We preach Christ as crucified." It is another sign of the same blindness that he treats the Reformation as if it established a certain difference between morality and religion. What the Reformation did was to establish the connection of morality with the Atonement. In the Catechism of Heidelberg the whole system of ethics is embraced under the article concerning gratitude. And so in the Confession of Basel we read: "We do not ascribe righteousness and satisfaction for our sins to work as a fruit of faith, but solely to true confidence and faith in the Blood of the Lamb of God, which was shed for the remission of our sins, for we freely confess that all things are given to us in Christ. Therefore believers are not to perform good works to make satisfaction for their sins, but only in order to manifest their gratitude for the great mercy which the Lord God has shown us in Christ." A deeper study of the conditions which caused the Reformation would have helped him to see that it was a reaction against self-righteousness which he condemns, that self-righteousness whose end is pride, or impotence, or recklessness. We read in the Confession of Augsburg, "That the doctrine of faith, which must be the chief of all in the Church, lay long unknown, as all must confess that in preaching there was the most profound silence concerning the righteousness of faith, and that only the doctrine of works was urged in churches." The result of preaching of the doctrine of works, by which some believe that the Church may be revived, was that the practice of the Evangelical Church fell into the deepest decay, ending in an entire and terrible denial of Christ and His Gospel. Mr. Strong speaks indeed of the barrier of sin being taken away, but he does not understand what was central alike to Apostolic and Reformation teaching, that in the reconciliation once made by the death of Christ, and not in the second reconciliation realised internally is the essential redeeming principle.

We have no space to work out this idea or to traverse the objectionable portion of Mr. Strong's teaching. Though unsatisfactory in his treatment of the Atonement and in the part of his book we have sketched, he is in harmony with the New Testament, with the Church, and with all the better thinking of our time, whether Christian or not. It cannot be too strongly said that the unconscious retreats into the old Socinianism which we have to lament here and there are not in the line of the serious thought and study of our time. As for the complaint that the Christian standard is too high, Mr. Strong meets it nobly. He says that the appeal to expect less is the most dangerous form in which the world calls upon us for our allegiance to it. "For we know how much there is still to do, and how slow the march of God's purpose seems to short-lived men, how far off the coming of the kingdom. But it has never been a mark of the spirit to hope and scheme only for what human foresight sees may easily be achieved. When the Lord pours out His Spirit, young men see visions and old men dream dreams, visions and dreams that rise like other dreams out of an experience actually attained in life and are prophetic of a fulness of triumph yet to come."

"GEOCENTRICISM": THE LATEST SCARECROW

WE may as well explain at once the hideous word which gives the title to these pages. In his new book, "Guesses at the Riddle of Existence," Mr. Goldwin Smith contends that those who believe in the Christian redemption believe that the earth is the centre of the universe. According to Mr. Smith, the Christian view of the world does not take into adequate account the insignificance of our earth in comparison with the vastness of the planetary system. We shall reply to Mr. Smith on this head, but ere doing so it may be worth while to answer from his own mouth some of his detailed objections to Christian doctrine. His early books were so occasional in their nature, they were published so long ago, that even very well-informed critics, like a writer in the *Guardian*, do not know them, and credit Mr. Goldwin Smith with a much greater degree of ignorance than he can rightly claim. They think, and the mistake is natural, that Mr. Smith approaches Christianity from the outside. What is true is that he has gone outside it.

In three little books published about the same time and under the same influence, there is, we believe, more genuine Christian passion than will be found in equal compass through the whole range of the Victorian literature. These three little books are Dora Greenwell's "The Patience of Hope," F. W. H. Myers's "St. Paul," and Goldwin Smith's "Does the Bible sanction American Slavery?" All three books were written under the inspiration of Josephine Butler. Since the volume referred to Mr. Goldwin Smith has written much, and his style is so brilliant, his moral ardour so contagious, that though he has adopted the strangest ways of publication, some readers have kept track of him and missed nothing that they could find out. He has written no book that will live. Indeed, it would be true to say that he has written no book at all. All his work is occasional. He has been a critic, a correspondent, a pamphleteer, a contributor, but he has never braced himself to the deliberate treatment of a great subject. He is himself an argument for that immortality which he has come to doubt, for it is hard to think that an intellect so wakeful as Goldwin Smith's should ever fall on sleep. One of his earliest and most effective pamphlets was written in reply to Mansel's Bampton Lectures, and is entitled "Rational Religion." From its pages we find that Mr. Smith was in 1861 a firm believer in Christianity, and a learned and enlightened student of theology. He was in the main a follower of Coleridge, whose thought, according to him, was the anchor by which the religious intellect of England had ridden out the storms of this tempestous age. He argued for Christianity from its effect in the regeneration of the world, and from the type of character displayed in the life of its founder. He was willing to concede the fact of miracle, finding miracle reasonable on the ground that the first believers naturally had such evidence as they could understand. Mr. Goldwin Smith talks now as if he had never read Coleridge, and the *Guardian* naturally supposes that Mr. Smith has been trained in the old theory of strict verbal inspiration, in which the Bible is a miracle and nothing else, and the ordinary conditions of authorship are in abeyance. It is true that Mr. Smith now argues as if that were so. Either, he says, the six days of creation must be rigidly maintained, as well as the precise literal truth of all the early narratives of Genesis, or the whole Bible is discredited. If any one suggests that there may be allegory in the opening chapters of Scripture, Mr. Smith says, "If it was from the Holy Spirit that this narrative emanated, how can the Holy Spirit have failed to let mankind know that they are allegories?" Such fatuities are almost incredible in a man who once at least knew a great deal better than that. Why, it is more than thirty-five years since Mr. Smith complained that Mansel insisted on the bare hard text of Scripture as if it were a brazen regulator thrust into the world by an almighty Power. It was Mr. Goldwin Smith who complained that Mansel's system drove you either to accept the literal accuracy of every part, or to reject the authority of the whole. He justly scouted the idea that a trivial discrepancy may deprive man of revelation and God. He said nobly: "If we can know God and know His voice, these difficulties are as nothing. If we cannot know God, they are death." Mr. Goldwin Smith now meddles a little with criticism, and he has a good deal to say against the Old Testament.

He regards it as a great burden which Christianity has to carry. He was wiser once. Nobody spoke more eloquently than he of the righteousness and pity of the Divine Word. No one spoke with more scathing scorn of those who attack the morality of the Old Testament, blind to the fact that the Jewish nation was not a miracle, but a people. No one pointed out more clearly the gradual spiritual elevation of the Old Testament, the way in which the essence of morality keeps growing through its pages. He showed that such a moral progress is what we must have expected to find, "unless it had been the design of Providence entirely to exempt the Jewish nation from all spiritual effort, and to make their religious history an automatic exhibition utterly disconnected with the general travailing of humanity, and alien to the sympathies of mankind." He now denies the Johannine authorship of the Fourth Gospel, but then he was able to show how in its concluding chapters we saw how divine and human love could be the same. Although Mr. Goldwin Smith has manifestly failed to study recent Biblical criticism, and although those parts of his book in which he refers to the subject may properly be called contemptible for their ignorance and unfairness, it is sufficient to say that on these subjects he may be invited to answer himself.

Mr. Smith has now come to doubt the immortality of the soul. It is impossible, he thinks, to find a decently cogent proof of a life to come. Here again we answer him out of his own mouth. He argued once that our moral life is the essence of our being, and that our moral life does not end when the body dies. "If," said he, "a single man can be found whose conscience, fairly interrogated, tells him or suffers him to act on the belief that the death of the body closes the moral account, and that when he is dead it will be all the same for him whether in his life he has done good or evil, I may think it possible to believe that there is no proof, except in Scripture, of the immortality of the soul." Now he has come to question all the arguments, but he does not willingly resign himself to the new situation. "A glory has passed from earth, for on every festal board in the community of terrestrial bliss will be cast the shadow of approaching death, and the sweeter life becomes, the more bitter death will be." Mr. Smith has not come to the comparative acquiescence of W. R. Greg in his later writings. Greg found that three score years and ten quenched the passionate desire for life. Weary with toil, satiated with pleasure, having had sufficient experience of those blessings of human affection which are mingled with such intense agonies, he found that renewed existence offered no inspiring charms, that he was tired of one life and felt scarcely equal to another, that he yearned most for rest, and the peace he could imagine easiest, because he knew it best, was the peace of sleep. This is not Mr. Goldwin Smith's as yet, but he, too, has come to believe with Greg that the faith in immortality is built rather upon a craving of nature than upon a grounded conviction, and that it has clinging to it the curse attaching to all illegitimate possessions. Yet Mr. Smith is not satisfied. Through all his career he has clung to faith in the moral order. One rock is still to him staringly above water, but he does not know how to save the ship that is drifting straight upon it from wreck and ruin. He does not understand, he cannot tell, how if we give up the belief in God, we shall be able to preserve the old morality. Neither can we. In old times Mr. Smith would have turned this inability into a splendid and positive argument for theism and Christianity.

But it is high time we came to the business of geocentricism. It takes us back to the days of our fathers, to the "Astronomical Discourses" of Dr. Chalmers and the literature they evoked, to the writings of Isaac Taylor and Whewell and Brewster. It should be noticed in the first place that Mr. Smith himself once saw and maintained with great eloquence that no arguments drawn from history can destroy Christianity. "No question," he said, "that concerns the validity of mere historical evidence can be absolutely vital to religion. For religion is a spiritual affection excited by nothing less than the assured presence of its Object. Christianity has been the life of the world for eighteen hundred years. It is the life of the world still. No serious attack has been made upon its essence. Reason is the creation of God, and it is not likely that He will be dethroned by the work of His own hands.' And in the same way science and its discoveries can never touch the life of Christianity. Christianity is friendly to all true science and history, but it is not of their order. It is impassive to all their attacks, it does not need their defence, it did not come from the mind of man, it descended from a higher region, and holds its inexpugnable place in the heart and conscience. But to come closer to the argument. There is to begin with no comparative measure between the infinite and the finite. Whatever the universe may be, no matter how our conception of the immensities be extended by further astronomical discoveries, it remains true that the universe is finite. It is not infinite any more than a drop of water is. Because our vision is limited and weak, it may seem to be infinite, but to the Infinite Being, as Coleridge says, the distance between the stars and systems is no more than that between particles of earth is to us. Hence every argument grounded on the supposition that mere vastness approximates infinity, and is more to God than comparative littleness, is from the very nature of the case a fallacy. Further, the measure of the spirit and the measure of matter are not the same. Pascal put the whole case in his pregnant sentence: "If the universe were to fall and crush me, I should be greater than the universe, for I should be conscious of defeat, and it would be unconscious of victory." The lustre of suns and constellations, whatever it may be, is nothing beside the glories of the human spirit. The universe, no matter how extended it may be, is dead. It cannot think, or feel, or imagine, or love. The child from whose mouth God has perfected praise is greater than the sun, greater than all the worlds which, though put together, are dumbly magnificent. And as the *Guardian* points out, Dr. Hutchison Stirling has shown that except to an eye and ear the whole system of things is simply an indefinite extension of stones vibrating in silence and in darkness. We ourselves make the marvels of the universe. Light is mere undulation of particles except to us. The music of the spheres itself is music only to an ear. Man exists in a universe of hustling and dancing atoms which are material through and through. The physical insignificance of man may be contrasted with the incomparable vastness of his surroundings only when it is forgotten that man is more than matter, and that matter, save in its relation to percipient beings, has no true existence.

These arguments have not been needed of late, because the belief in the existence of thinking beings in other worlds is less strong than it was. Isaac Taylor in his "Saturday Evening" has a fine essay, entitled, "The State of Seclusion." In this he points out that we are insulated from other worlds in order that our probation may be more completely secured. He argues that if we saw from this world all the consequences of good and evil as manifested in the innumerable worlds which, he thought, were replete with intellectual and moral life, we should be driven into virtue, not led into it, by a consideration of its results. But God hides these from us that our great choice may be a matter of voluntary consent. Even if there are intellectual and moral beings in other worlds, that does not concern us. We do not know it, we do not know them. If they exist we know nothing of their conditions. What we do know is that into our world the Son of God has come, and that in our world the pure in heart may see God. Our Lord and His Apostles were never daunted, far less overwhelmed, by the immensity of the universe. He who stood behind the tremendous curtain of creation, who knew the ineffable secret, who beheld with open face the glory of the Lord, promised the same vision to all who should trust Him. His Apostle said: "All these things shall be dissolved. The heavens shall pass away with a great noise; the elements shall melt with fervent heat; the earth also and the works that are thereon shall be burnt up." But though the starry splendours be folded up like a vesture and changed, we are to survive them. We are not to be dissolved. We, according to His promise, look for new heavens and a new earth wherein dwelleth righteousness. We see beyond us the enduring realities that last when this majestic universe, which was the nursery of the budding soul, has passed like a dream, and when the glories of the visible creation are as toys that have been surmounted and put away. We may see, as Apostles did, the invisible order. Our thoughts may be with the enduring—with the great High Priest set over the house of God, the perpetual liturgy of the world of spirits, the Throne behind the veil.

www.ingramcontent.com/pod-product-compliance
Lightning Source LLC
Chambersburg PA
CBHW030016240426
43672CB00007B/971